The Dance of Life

Dorothy Buck

PARAGON HOUSE

NEW YORK

Acknowledgments

I am grateful to Ewert H. Cousins and Richard Payne for their encouragement and support in preparing this manuscript, and to the community of Carmelite Sisters in Barrington, Rhode Island for their hospitality and continuing prayers.

Published by Paragon House
2 Hammarskjold Plaza
New York, New York

Cover Design by Kathy Daniels

Library of Congress Cataloging-in-Publication Data

Buck, Dorothy.
    The dance of life.

    Bibliography: p.
    1. Dancing. 2. Dancing—Philosophy. I. Title.
GV1594.B78   1987   793.3   86-30324

ISBN 0-913757-52-7 (pbk.)

Contents

II

The Experience of Dance

III

A Contemplative Theory of Dance

To my children, Ariane and Raoul
and my father, Martin
with love.

I

What is Dance?

I believe that dance is the oldest, noblest, and most cogent of the arts.
I believe that dance is the most perfect symbol of the activity of God and
His angels.
I believe that dance has the power to heal, mentally and physically.
I believe that true education in the art of dance is education of the whole
man.

Ted Shawn

1

Dance as Primitive Human Expression

Agnes de Mille calls art, "symbols through which people communicate what lies beyond ordinary speech...art is communication on the deepest and most lasting level."[1] It is a need which human beings cannot live without. Art transcends surface qualities and reaches to inner depths.

We live in a world of images. Even our thoughts are a series of word images. Our memories are imaginary pictures of human experiences of life. Communication is translating thought images into word symbols which others can understand. Beyond the image is the idea, or message, which is conveyed via the word symbol. We see creation in beautiful forests, turbulent ocean waves, and fields of blooming flowers. These are the images that reflect our environment. Behind these tangible images of our physical world, however, is a deeper reality that binds us to one another, and puts us at one with creation itself.

The difference between self-consciousness and self-transcendence is revealed when self-awareness expands to include all humanity. When self-expression becomes universal and timeless we have art, rather than egotism. All great human works of art are timeless; they defy social and cultural change, and remain meaningful to generation after generation. Artists strive for freedom of expression by laboriously mastering techniques which becomes secondary when the artist can transcend them with a sense of abandonment. Accepting the necessary demands of self-discipline requires something other than technical mastery or skill. Once the technical skill is acquired that "something" is the result. Now the creative process can begin. Transcendence makes one reach beyond the human and strive to find in oneself what is at once unique and universal.

Communication is a primary motivation for all forms of art. Dance is the oldest art form because movement is the natural response of life to creation. Primitive peoples spontaneously responded to internal body movements and inner pulses of life. They imitated the rhythms and visual movements in their environment. Movement was the natural expression of deep emotional responses. These identified human beings as within the natural rhythms of nature.

Basic human needs are evident in terms of nature and natural rhythm. The movement of the universe has pre-designed our human response. We eat, sleep, work and play in tune with our environment in the cycles of the day, night, months, years, weather and crops. In order to cope with the "magic" of their universe, primitives expressed their needs in ritual movements to the elements. Ultimately, they imitated these "gods" in stylized dances. The primitive basis for movement expression is found in rhythm. Joost A.M. Meerloo, in his essays on creative instinct, states,

> in the dance man's earliest existence is revealed. . . rhythm and gesture somewhere reverberate man's nirvanic yearnings [his instinct to return to the experience of the womb]. . . The embryo lives in a continuous internal sound world, hearing the pulsations of its own heart beat and the maternal heart beat. Thus, the child, before birth, lives in an overwhelming syncopated sound world.[2]

4

This world of sound and rhythm that we are in tune with before our own birth indicates that sound and rhythm are basic to all humanity, leading us to cosmic realities.

In *Harmony of the Spheres*, the Greek philosopher Pythagoras "looked at the universe as a symphony of waves and rhythms all together forming the music of God."[3] George Leonard described an interesting experiment done at Yale University:

> Johannes Keplar, the seventeenth century astronomer, in discovering the laws of planetary motion, worked out each planet's "song" in terms of its orbit around the sun. Willie Ruff, an assistant professor of music, and John Rodgers, a professor of geology, took Keplar's laws and musical notations and applied them to the motion of the planets as projected over a one hundred year period starting December 31, 1976. They fed this information into a computer connected to a music synthesizer. What emerged was a thirty minute tape representing one hundred years of planetary motion. It came out as a spectacular if somewhat dizzying piece of music . . .[4]

Leonard speaks of the underlying rhythm that sustains life. By exploring the nature of rhythm, harmony, and synchronization we shall see how the artist is in tune with them. In terms of dance and primitive peoples, Meerloo writes, "Dancing man can be in tune with the universe when his dancing leads him to the pinnacle of ecstacy and unification, but he can also be out of tune, lost in the depth of confusion and bewilderment."[5] Primitive peoples found a kind of "magic" in the relationship of rhythm and gesture to interactions with both other people and animals. This developed into the ritual dances that can still be seen today in primitive tribal societies. Dances ward off dangers and gain power over animals and natural elements. Ritual dances are a manifestation of

> man's will to overcome his fears and to become master of his fate. Many initiation dances of primitive tribes and early religious rites represent this very archaic magic strategy of man's fight against, as well as his submission to, the rhythm of the world. Initiation, becoming an adept, gathering

knowledge, and dancing one's own free rhythm, are the beginnings of the liberation of man from being merely a biological and instinctual animal.[6]

Communication and community are keys to solving many of the ills that plague our society. Overcoming anxiety, loneliness, and separation, through community activity, group therapy, social clubs, and organizations meet the needs of people and are common in our society. Very early in the history of civilization, primitive people discovered the value of rhythmic movement. As a religious rite, it is capable of relieving a sense of isolation and fear of death. Sacred war dances, whirling dervishes, shamans, and even the orgy, developed out of a need to express emotions through rhythmic movement. In more civilized society, Eastern mystics experience ecstatic holy union with the universe through the use of rhythmic breathing in unison. Both primitive and more civilized experiences of ecstasy are an expression of a human urge to "surrender to the greater pulsations of the universe. It is only man who makes a creative art out of his urge to rhythmic motion."[7]

2

Life Force

According to the dictionary life is the quality that distinguishes a vital and functional being from a dead body or inanimate matter. Force is active power, strength or energy of exceptional degree, or an influence that causes motion, or a change of motion. Without movement there is no life. Life is evolutionary. The unfolding of life assumes growth, change, and therefore movement. The animating quality of life stems from energy, or active power. This energy is a primary force to which all life responds, and from which all life evolves.

Life force is a synthesis of motivating factors. It underlies the power of creativity, sometimes producing extraordinary innovation in those individuals whose vision compels them to reveal their insight to others. It operates in all human beings. With expanded consciousness and increased awareness, it can stimulate previously untapped creative energy. By allowing this energy to grow into a powerful force, life is set into motion, transforming ordinary human capacities into the extraordinary.

It is interesting to reflect on an ancient belief that

the spirit was essentially the life of the body, or a kind-of life force which assumed spatial and corporeal form at birth or after conception, and left the dying body again after the final breath . . . It was considered timeless and thus immortal.[1]

C.G. Jung compares the root meanings of words that gave names to the soul.

In Latin, Greek and Arabic the names given to the soul are related to the notion of moving air . . . and this also is why the primitive point of view endows the soul with an invisible breath-body. Since breath is the sign of life, breath is taken for life, as are also movement and moving force.[2]

Jung points out that primitive peoples experienced the psyche as the source of life. The psyche contained a life of its own; it was the spirit of motivation, and objectively real. We see evidence of this concept in the Hebrew scriptures: God is pictured "breathing" life into Adam in the book of Genesis.

Jung envisioned the collective unconscious as having a certain objective aspect. This suggests that our egoconsciousness grows out of our unconscious reality. If we were totally able to integrate our unconscious into our conscious awareness, we would find ourselves at-one-with the very source of life itself. This driving force toward integration—the natural quest for wholeness—is the necessary ingredient for a true vocation. Marilyn Ferguson says, "vocation is the process of making one's way toward something. It is a direction more than a goal."[3] She calls vocation a "calling", and so do I. Quoting Jung, she says,

Speaking of his own experience, Jung said, "Vocation acts like a law from God from which there is no escape." The creative person is over-powered, captive of and driven by a demon. Unless one assents to the power of the inner voice, the personality cannot evolve. "Although we often mistreat those who listen to this voice," he said, "still they become our legendary heroes."[4]

8

The "calling" or vocation is an extension of a primitive life force. It is the energy that impels persons to listen to the inner voice, often against overwhelming obstacles. It assumes faith not only in one's own creative vision, but in the energy that underlies it. This life force of creative energy moves us to reach beyond the conscious toward transcendent life expression. Henri Nouwen speaks of the vision and discipline of the artist as parallel to the contemplation and ministry of the contemplative religious. The artist is a true contemplative, if contemplative is to "see" and "know" what others do not "see" and "know", and if the artist's ministry is to make visible what he does "see" and "know". "A contemplative is one who sees things for what they really are, who sees the real connections . . . a movement from opaqueness to transparency."[5] For the artist, life force is the energy that compels creativity, combined with a need to reveal one's vision to others.

Ferguson writes,

> Many artists have said that when life itself becomes fully conscious, art, as we know it, will vanish. Art is only a stopgap, an imperfect effort to wrest meaning from an environment where nearly everyone is sleepwalking.[6]

The most natural and universal desire of human beings is to communicate. Without language as we know it, primitive people used their bodies as an instrument for communication. Self-expression is essentially a need to relate, not only to others, but to all of creation. Our earliest experience of life in infancy exemplifies a most primitive means of expression. Like our pre-historic ancestors, infantile expression is based on rhythm, sound, and movement in various natural ways. Only we rise beyond a primitive natural urge to make use of our special human gift—the power of creativity. By participating in the creative process itself, we share in the reality of transcendence and expand our quality of life. Psychologically, the movements of self-expression, relationship, and communication are essential to the mental health and well being of all persons. In our own quest for wholeness, dancers use their bodies as expressive instruments, as primitive societies have done through the ages. We reveal our deepest selves in a language without words. Tapping into a source of energy, or primitive life force, we share our creations. This gift of creative energy belongs to all persons and is meant to set us free. As dancers, our freedom communicates the life force within each one of us. Through dance, we are free to participate in life and relate to all of creation. Dance expresses what is most human through the natural synthesis of rhythm, sound and movement.

3

Religious Expression: The Language of Dance

> Probably all art loses its deeper justification when divorced from religion. But all dance is a rite and has retained its ritualistic roots even in such stylized forms as the ballet. The dancer in our day may have forgotten his ties with man's early beginnings, but he can never deny them.[1]

It is difficult to imagine conscious existence without verbal expression. Only in early infancy are human beings unable to think in word symbols. Then our relationship to the environment is still governed by rhythm, sound, and movement. Language soon begins to infiltrate our pre-consciousness. It overpowers the instinctual and infantile physical expressions of our inner feelings and needs. In pre-historic societies, however, the human body was the only available means of self-expression and communication. Relationship to the environment was experienced as crucial to identity and survival. Through another art form, primitive peoples left us a wonderful legacy to the unique developmental process in human beings. In the drawings of cave dwellers we find the earliest written signs and

11

symbols. They reveal communities of people—dancing! For primitive people dance was the same as thinking and feeling. Today we might call their response to life "holistic". Their whole mental, spiritual, and physical being demanded communication and their bodies became their instrument of expression. Their relationship with nature was also distinctively "holistic". They intimately responded to and reflected their environment by becoming a part of it. Entering into creation itself, they became one within it. Primitive dance was religious, fully integrated into life activities. Totally spontaneous, yet always purposeful, it expressed every facet of living, from birth to death. Primitive peoples danced wars, marriages, hunting, healing, and dispelling evil spirits. All warriors, chiefs, and priests danced. They sought control over natural elements through the power of their ritualistic dancing. The supernatural was conceived as a living force, and primitive people identified with it. They possessed the earth by stamping their feet. They spontaneously, and fully, expressed their feelings with a freedom of movement that recalls the vocational yearnings of all true artist-dancers. They never danced merely for the sake of dancing. Instead, dancing was the celebration of their whole experience of life. They danced because they were dance. Complete freedom of movement identified the meaning of life. Ritualistic movement was the earliest expression of a primitive life force and religion.

Symbolic meaning is the key to dance as ritual. Early biblical society was not very different from more ancient peoples. The Old Testament is full of references to dancing. With the development of civilization, self-expression through dancing became a form of worship. Movements reflected the qualities attributed to God. Thus, it was natural for the Israelites to express their religious feelings in terms of sacred dancing. As they entered the Temple for festivals and holy days, they danced the Psalms to praise their God. We incorporate the cultural aspects of our lives and national traditions into our religions. Early Christians interjected the diverse customs of people throughout the Middle East into their religious ritual. Where dancing was culturally acceptable, it remained in the liturgy. It was rejected from the liturgy where it was considered pagan.

Much Christian spirituality has tended to separate the body from the soul. As he labored to enhance the spiritual aspects of human life, Saint Augustine turned tradition away from the body as an acceptable expression of religious feelings. He set the climate of thought in the fifth century for many future generations of Christians. Great choruses of Psalms, and even Christmas carols were meant to be danced and sung. Only the Eucharistic Liturgy of Eastern Orthodox Christianity has consistently maintained elements of the original celebration in movement and gesture. At times in the Medieval and Renaissance periods, dance and the arts in general, became acceptable in the Western Church. However, the Reformation stressed the written word as the approach to life and religion. Many Protestant denominations considered all forms of dance sinful.

In the twentieth century, movement is again returning to our religious celebrations. Dance becomes an acceptable expression of our relationship within God when it is carefully integrated into the liturgy, or experienced in prayer seminars. This brief religious history of dance clearly identifies a dichotomy between our own experience and primitive religious ritual. In order to fully appreciate dance in its highly developed contemporary forms, we must return to the primordial source of inspiration. Integration of life forces creates a sense of harmony in the universe. Our Judeo-Christian ancestors experienced a relationship with God beyond the concepts of primitive deities. Still, they embrace God through primitive human gestures and symbolic movement. Symbolic movement is the language of dance. It is a natural means of reaching beyond ourselves to the transcendent. By adding gesture to language, word symbols are given an intensity of meaning which can become a powerfully moving force. Symbolic movement and pantomime help satisfy our human desire for the freedom of self expression. Through this basic and primitive form of communication, contemporary dancers continue to transcend our highly developed verbal languages. The religious ritual of dancing lives an abundant life in the midst of our secular, diverse, and sophisticated contemporary dance performances.

13

4

Music in Primitive Ritual Dancing

> We are so constituted that we yawn when others yawn, laugh
> when they laugh, weep when they weep, feel sympathetic
> muscular strains when we watch others struggling under heavy
> loads, and are stimulated to dance when they dance.[1]

The relationship between movement and music in primitive
ritual dancing becomes clear when we realize that primitive peoples
were immersed in an environment of sound. They imitated the
sounds along with the rhythms. They vocally responded to the
stamping of their own feet and the sound of whirling and ecstatic
movements. Joyful noises often accompany our joy filled movements. The first sounds of song accompanied primitive ritual dancing. As the rhythm of the movements gained in intensity, spectators
picked up both the beat of the rhythm and its vocal accompaniment.
Today, we are familiar with an extraordinarily refined and developed
relationship of music and dance. It began with this natural synthesis
of movement, rhythm and sound. At the primitive level, human
potential for rhythmic movement and sound is not so different from

other members of the animal kingdom. However, human beings, with their flexible hands and creative imaginations, soon fashioned instruments to accentuate the rhythm and accompany their dance and song. Their instruments finally went beyond the sounds of nature and even beyond the scope of human voice. Our contemporary societies separate music and dance into two distinct art forms. When music is written specifically for dancing, these primitive relationships provide the essential ingredients. It will reflect the rhythmic pulse of dancing bodies and remain in tune with the accompanying sound of human voices. Tribal dances were intended to evoke "magical" power over animals and natural elements. By participating in the dance, the tribal group accentuated its conscious strength and power. Human beings first experienced the principle of strength, in unity of purpose, and power, in mass group participation, in the sounds and rhythms of their primitive ritual dancing.

In order to fully grasp where we are as dancers today, we need to look at the early history of dance through the experience of our primitive ancestors. Even a dance form as stylistic as the Classical Ballet remains in tune with the basic nature of dance. The sense of being connected to the sounds and rhythms of nature through symbolic movement arouses our recognition of a movement in our own society. The integration of our mental, physical, and spiritual experience of existence into a "holistic" unity, has become a popular theme. It seems strange that, in the name of civilization, we have traveled so far away from the holistic, natural experience of our ancient ancestors. Now, we must recapture what we have always known at some deeper level. Our first experience of communication still remains our most effective means of reaching beyond our highly developed language systems. Physical expression of our essential humanity enhances, and often surpasses, our limited vocabularies of words. Even in literature and theatre, we rely on the symbolic meaning of image and movement as a primitive life force that continues to reveal who we are, how we relate, and ultimately, how we transcend ourselves. Dancers still experience their connection with nature and strive to "become" dance. When we succeed, dance becomes a means of communication and reaches into the depths of our common humanity. We find ourselves participating in the basic qualities of natural, universal, and transcendent human experience. The religious rite of dance continues to inspire the creativity of contemporary dancers and choreographers. Our bodies sing the song in our hearts. We share an ancient experience of power, and the unity inherent in communal movement, with our primordial ancestors.

5

Life Rhythm

Our urge to rhythmic motion corresponds to that same urge in all living creatures. Nature tends toward perfect rhythm; it takes far more energy to move against a common flow than to move in the same direction. In terms of dance, this is easy to understand. In the beginning, dancers use a great deal of energy and effort in training the human body. This energy builds the strength and coordination necessary to move in many different ways at once. As the coordination and muscular strength develops, it takes increasingly less energy to realize the required movements. Thus, the more technique we achieve, the easier the most difficult movements become. Apparently this is a reality of nature, and a universal phenomenon.

George Leonard uses the word "entrainment" to describe natural synchronization. This can be seen "whenever two or more oscillators in the same field are pulsing at nearly the same time. They tend to 'lock-in' so that they are pulsing at exactly the same time."[1] This kind of synchronization is a necessity for our human internal mechanisms to operate properly. Even without our awareness, the rhythm of our breathing, the rhythmic pulse of energy in the heart beat, and the interaction of internal systems keep us alive as they cooperate in a state of constant motion. The relationship of movements in our external environment is still more interesting. Leonard describes an experiment which indicates a natural entrainment of person to person as they speak to one another. The imperceptible bodily movements that occur in the speaker are discerned as simultaneous movements in the listener. This is not a response. Instead there is a sharing of rhythm, or a oneness with the other. In other words, rhythm is not something added to our communication, but rather something linking, and underlying communication. Leonard explains that "a new born infant, like a normal adult, moves synchronously with the pattern of the mother's voice . . . The infant is born already connected with the fundamental rhythms that hold us all together."[2]

This rhythm, or synchronization of life, can be illustrated from the cosmic to the microcosmic. It is the universal connection. This is the symbolic Shiva (The Great Lord of India) who holds the universe in an eternal dance of life. The relationships that create life rhythm are not isolated events or entities. They are the essential factor determining the creative flow of rhythmic energy. The synthesis of many parts of a whole creates something new. A new creation cannot be predicted by any single one of its parts. The natural movement toward synthesis in nature reflects our own natural movement toward wholeness. The more sensitive we are in relationship to our own environment, the more potential creativity exists. In the bringing together of various energies, we produce something more vibrant, more perfect, or more alive. Sensitive artists pick-up on all kinds of energy sources. By recognizing them as part of themselves, they are able to create a further wholeness. For example, dance is transformed into art when dancers recognize the internal rhythm inherent to all pieces of music. They relate to the beat and pulse, and pick up the subtle internal musical rhythms. The synthesis with their own internal rhythms creates a new realization of the music. Rhythm is a part of entrainment. It is a tuning-in to the flow of natural rhythm in our environment and within our own persons. We say that different life styles have their own rhythm. We adjust our own natural, instinctive rhythm of life to fit into that pattern. It includes a relationship to internal energy and external environment. The paradigm remains true as long as there is sufficient awareness of individual life rhythm and its collective similarity with others. It must remain in-tune with the external environment. If any of the pattern is altered at any of its points of relationship, there must be a shift. Marilyn Ferguson describes paradigm shifts as responsible for both social and personal transformation. Temperament, personality, emotional flexibility, drive, character, and other facets of the human psyche are intertwined with developing talent and nurturing creativity. Recognizing our personal rhythm paradigm and being aware of its potentially vast range of flexibility, can only increase our opportunities for creativity and openness to innovation.

The call to dance is a response to a primitive urge to rhythmic motion. It is an unavoidable internal rhythm of life that dictates the will and choices of the person. Jonas Salk, who discovered the first polio vaccine, is quoted by Ferguson as saying, " 'I have frequently felt that I have not so much chosen but that I have been chosen.' He added that things he felt compelled to do despite his rationalizations proved immensely rewarding."[3] We grow in-tune with our own internal life rhythm by learning to recognize its subtleties and patterns. Developing a sense of freedom and acceptance of change, both internally and externally, is a good beginning. As dancers we learn to relate to music in the same way. By doing so, we transform music into dance. All music has its own life rhythm and subtle internal variations. So does every dance, every dancer, and every choreographer. The music itself is a reflection of the life rhythm of the composer. This is true of all artistic expression. Collaboration of life rhythms is therefore essential to artistic endeavor. We can therefore say that life rhythm is a response—an inner voice. It acts like an urge, or motivating stimulant. Life rhythm is the source of energy, a response to energy, as well as a synthesis of energies.

Intuition is another aspect of rhythm. We easily relate intuition to creativity. It also relates to rhythm. Entrainment is unconscious and therefore intuitive. It involves unconscious simultaneous

21

movements that are imperceptible even to a discerning eye. We intuitively operate out of our own life rhythm in relation to others. Rhythm is so basic to personality that our intuition for it is generally accurate. Training rhythmic response is only increasing our awareness of an already existing life rhythm. We sense the rhythm of music just as we know our own natural body rhythms. That "knowing", with increased awareness, is what can cause a dancer to become the music or the dance. Primitive societies were so in-tune with movement that they became the dance and discovered a means of communication. That intuitive knowing is an expression of the reality of life rhythm.

6

The European History of Ballet

The development of civilization affected human creativity. It brought dance from a natural and very human ritualistic expression of life to a refined and progressively more stylized, formal expression. As a result, dance has passed through periods of conflict concerning its most essential qualities. We have created a highly technical art form. It struggles to maintain a balance between the extremes of an essentially spiritual nature and its extraordinary technical development. Prominent figures in the history of Classical Ballet have consistently raised its technical standard and artistic quality. Yet dance remains a viable expression of a primordial need to transcend ourselves.

Relationship is a key to human creativity. The broader our life experience, the greater our ability to absorb it into our art forms. In Chapter Five, we described how relating rhythmic energies potentially creates new forms of expression, based on a knowledge of classical systems and traditional art. The freedom that we strive for comes with our increasing intuitive sense for the truth and nature of complementary life rhythms. The ability to tap sources of energy and relate them to one another, through an artistic medium, is part of the process in human creativity. The great artists and innovations in the development of Classical Ballet suggest parallels with nature. We spoke of a rhythmic process that tends toward harmony and synchronization. The history of dance exemplifies our human striving for unity and integration. Artists transform life experience into universal expressions of life rhythm. They remind us of the vast potential we share for human creative expression. Individually, we are each unique expressions of our common humanity. Because we are who we are, we do what we do. Thus infinite possibilities for new forms of dance expression continue to transform movement into art through the ages. As each new generation builds upon the innovations of the past, it reflects human progress.

In an effort to communicate their feelings and experience of life, primitive people used movement to express their relationship to others, the environment, and ultimately, to God. Dance developed from a primitive and holistic expression to a highly sophisticated and theatrical performing art. As we shall see, the essence of dance remains natural, universal, and transcendent. A study of the history and development of Classical Ballet will inevitably lead us, through its human artists, back to those essential qualities. The trends that govern our historical progress also reveal developing threads of artistic creativity. Agnes de Mille points out that the cultures and civilizations that most directly shaped our present Western civilization were the five Mediterranean civilizations of the Bronze and Iron Ages: the Egyptian, Hebrew, Greek, Roman, and Mesopotamian.

The Iron Age men were horsemen and athletes who rose to the dignity of their achievements.

> The Bronze Age man was aware of beauty, not only as magic, but as a quality in itself. . .Beauty of line was a vital factor in his life; posture and gesture were valued for appearance as well as for meaning. Visual patterns were devised because their form gave pleasure. . .a step beyond mere rhythm patterns. Dances became a sequence of movement in which over-all design played a leading part.[1]

24

We have already mentioned the place of dance in the ancient Hebrew and early Christian traditions. These are our ancestors in terms of religious thought.

The decadence of the Roman Empire was responsible for turning the beauty and refinement of the Greek art of dancing into vulgarity. With the development of Christian values, religious dance was almost entirely rejected. The effect on dance, as liturgical religious ritual, is felt even today. During the early Middle Ages, there was no theatre nor dance. Then religious plays began to be performed—mysteries, miracles and moralities. They dealt with the religious mysteries and stories of the Old and New Testaments. Folk dancing continued in Europe in the Middle Ages, often only an unrefined and crude form of peasant dancing. In our culture, national folk dances are all that remain of ancient tribal ritual. These continue to affirm our emotional oneness, common heritage, and fundamental fellowship as human beings.[2]

Between the 12th and 14th centuries the nobility replaced the earthiness of the crude folk dance with the theatrical court dance. Here we can begin to trace the beginning of Classical Ballet as we know it today. In the 16th century the *commedia dell'arte* troupes began to appear in the provinces of France and Italy. At the same time, great pageants designed after Roman spectacles began to be staged and danced by members of the courts. These pageants mark the beginning of a technique and style that became one of the longest unbroken traditions in Western Theatre.

The early history of the Classical Ballet becomes clearer if we examine some of the inherent qualities of traditional art forms. According to Seyyed Hossein Nasr art is

> traditional not because of its subject matter, but because of its conformity to cosmic laws of forms, to the laws of symbolism, to the formal genius of the particular spiritual universe in which it has been created, its hieratic style, its conformity to the nature of the material used, and finally, its conformity to the truth within the particular domain of reality with which it is concerned. . .[3]

There is a pattern in human development that traditionally places human beings in the world as theomorphic creatures. Our art, from primitive expression to the contemporary, reflects our spirituality. Historically, dance progressively moves away from these "holistic" concepts. The laws that govern the basic principles of dance, however, remain the truth of human nature. Nasr continues,

> Traditional art is concerned with the truths contained in the tradition of which it is the artistic and formal expression. . . Traditional art, moreover, is functional in the most profound sense of this term, namely, that it is made for a particular use whether it be the worshipping of God in a liturgical act, or [an implement] for eating a meal. It is, therefore, utilitarian but not with the limited meaning of utility identified with purely earthly man in mind. Its utility concerns pontifical man for whom beauty is as essential a dimension of life, and a need, as the house that shelters man during the winter cold. . . In traditional art there is a blending of art and utility which makes every object of traditional art [providing it belongs to a thriving traditional civilization not in the stage of decay] something at once useful and beautiful.[4]

In 1661 the palace of Versailles was built for performance because of Louis XIV's interest in the dance. Known as the Sun King, he was a dancer himself. He created the Academy of Dance that still exists today at the Paris Opera. From France, to Italy and Russia, the Classical Ballet developed a tradition. This tradition continues to be handed down from teacher to pupil, and generation to generation. The innovations of individuals carrying on the tradition, and developing it, has created a Western art form with virtually no nationality. Ballet history is really a history of teachers, students and choreographers. A brief treatment of some of the renowned personalities responsible for the early development of the Classical Ballet follows.

We begin with Noverre, one of the first Ballet Masters of the French Academy. He brought Ballet to a level of scientific foundation described in his book, *Letters on Dancing*, written in 1760.

After Noverre came three generations of the Vestris family, from 1760-1842. It is interesting that there is a tradition of families handing the Classical Ballet tradition from one generation to the next, just as in many other professions and trades. After the Vestris family came Didelot, whose disciple was the famous Petipa (1822-1910). In 1803, Blasis formulated Noverre's technique in Milan. With his treatise on *The Art of Dancing*, he became known as the Father of the Classical Ballet. His pupil was Lepris, who in turn taught Cecchitti, an Italian technician whose discipline is taught to this day. In Russia, the Dance Academy was founded by Princess Ann and brought to St. Petersburg by Katherine the Great (1762-1796).[5]

La Scala, in Milan, Italy became the greatest ballet theatre in all of Europe. In 1812, Salvatore Vigano became the Ballet Master.

> He mounted works that unified music, dancing and mime as Noverre had never been able to do. Vigano regarded mime as the expression of "the movement of the soul; it is the language of all peoples, of all ages and times. It depicts better than words extremes of joy and sorrow. . . It is not sufficient for me to please the eyes," he said. "I wish to involve the heart."[6]

And one hundred years later,

> a young dancer and choreographer, Michel Fokine, who in 1905 created for the ballerina, Anna Pavlova, the short lyric dance, "the Dying Swan", rebelled against the omnipotence of "tradition". Like Noverre and Vigano before him Fokine aimed at unification of dancing, music, and design. He asserted that dancing was interpretive—expressive. "The ballet must no longer be made up of numbers, entries and so on . . . Ballet must have complete unity of expression, a unity which is made up of harmonious blending of the three elements, music, painting and plastic art."[7]

Underlying these quotations is one of the struggles that greatly influenced the development of dance as an art form. It is impossible to separate the history of Ballet from its aesthetics. The history consists of periods of great technical discovery and development, followed by an innovative Ballet Master who absorbs these discoveries into choreography. Technique is transformed into art. Thus, just as scientific discoveries must be interpreted for application to human needs, so dance technique must also find its expression in the realm of human need. Quoting the words of such influential masters of the Ballet as Salvatore Vigano and Michel Fokine focuses on the intense and serious quality of their personalities that was reflected in their work. Their vision was extreme in their day. They applied a high standard of aesthetic qualities to dance, emphasizing harmony and unity of complementary art forms. They spoke in poetic terms of their concepts of dance. The movement of the soul, involvement of the heart, and harmonious blending of the arts are all expressions that rise up from the depths of our own humanity.

Balanchine explains the meaning of classic and romantic in ballet history. These terms have a distinctive sense in relation to the development of Classical Ballet.

> The word classic when applied to ballet is not the contrary of romantic. It applies to a rigorous vocabulary of steps and movements capable of infinite variation, and a system of instruction that makes such variation, possible for individual dancers. Classic ballets can be romantic, realistic, or mythological in subject matter. The classic dance is the dictionary of ballet and, as a method of instruction, it is also its grammar: basic steps and movements that must be learned and mastered if the student is to become an instrument of its possibilities. Ballets that we call Romantic are a kind of classical ballet. . . What we recognize as Romanticism in ballet, was romantic in subject, temper and mood. . . [expressed] in the vocabulary of the classic dance. . . What is classic in ballet is what has developed over the years. . . What is romantic is a period through which that development passed.[8]

Classic, in this sense, means academic and constructed within certain laws. It pertains to a definite form. Each form remains within the realm of a traditional system of theory and technique. This allows the greatest flexibility as a point of departure for superimposing styles, personal interpretation, and artistic innovation. All traditional art forms are based on a classic system. The system becomes the vocabulary from which "new words" evolve. All classic systems also become excellent mediums for reflecting the culture, technology, and psychology, as well as the personal and social transformation of modern society.

Balanchine continues,

> Romanticism was responsible for revolutionary innovations on classic technique, and in the subject matter of ballets. Its desire for ethereal creatures caused dancers for the first time to rise on their toes, introduced the white ballet costume so familiar to us in *Giselle, Swan Lake* and *Les Sylphides*, and caused the expansion of the dance vocabulary to meet the expressive requirements of elfin, unattainable heroines and heroes who aimed at, and so seldom secured, permanent happiness. As it contrasted real life with fantasy, the Romantic Ballet naturalized the pastoral theme that dominated earlier ballet. . . The Romantic Ballet dominated the classic dance from about 1820 to 1870. After this time, what we recognize as the great classical ballets, *Swan Lake, Sleeping Beauty* etc., were created on the basis of a new uncovered, unconcealed technique and a more exacting dance discipline. Thus, unlike literature, music and the other arts, ballet's great period of classicism came after the development of romanticism. [9]

7

Classical Music and Dance

The relationship of music and dance accentuates the interconnectedness of all art forms and helps us understand their universal appeal. The relationship of dance to music is vital to our understanding of dance. Classical form in dance is related to classical form in music. Form, in both music and dance, is the structure, the way the music or dance is put together. There are some basic rules concerning the particular combinations of notes in music, and combinations of movements in dance. The form, in dance, depends upon the desired rhythm and visual effect in direct relationship to the quality of the musical form.

According to Hugo Leichtentritt, there are specific

> laws of proportion and symmetry dominating all music to such a degree that every musician is subject to them unconsciously... The more he is affected, the greater his innate talent is... The musical talent, the organic working of the musical mind becomes manifest in its instinct for these proportions. This instinct for shaping means talent. Art adds

to this subconscious activity of the mind the more precise, conscious knowledge of the laws of structure.[1]

Talented dancers respond to the laws of proportion and symmetry in music which relate to similar laws in Classical Ballet. Leichtentritt describes "Form" versus "forms" in music. His description relates to the structure in dance as well. He writes,

> Form as structural concept, idea, belongs to the permanently valid, immutable fundamental properties of music. The various forms, however, are the temporal, transient application of the unchangeable idea of Form. Form is related to the forms like the platonic idea, the ideal archetype, to the real objects, the single images of the idea. Form is elemental, organic, abstract; the forms are the concrete, practical samples, shaped by artistic handicraft. The concept of Form remains permanently, the specific forms change from time to time. In fact, there is neither a modern or an old-fashioned form. . . Whenever the listener is struck by vivid sound, logical development, characteristic color, true temperament, real expression, it matters little to him whether these qualities are manifest in the form of a passacagalia, a fugue, a sonata, a song a chain of variations. And inversely, the most interesting, novel form is worthless without the impression of spiritual vitality. Form might be compared to daylight, revealing the shape and nature of all objects, qualities that cannot be observed in nocturnal darkness.[2]

In both classical music and classical dance, therefore, Form is conformity to cosmic laws, to the nature of the sound, and to the rhythmical structure in the music or dance. It governs the initial construction in both. However, the forms, shaped by the artist, depend entirely on an instinctual talent for the truth inherent in the musical Form. This instinctual talent in dance is seen when the truth inherent in the musical Form is applied to dance or enhanced by it. Classical dancers strive to train their bodies to become perfect instruments for the dance. Simultaneously, they develop their instinctual response to the truth of the music to which they dance.

Generally, the classical training of body movements correspond to the formal structure of music. Movements are designed or phased in both tempo and quality to the nature of the musical accompaniment. By the time a dancer has mastered the technical aspects of the classical dance, the body responds quite naturally to the contrasts and variations in the music. Classical in dance refers to a system of word symbols and corresponding movements; in contrast, classical in music refers to a period in its development. In the sense that it indicates a particular style and formal structure, however, music can also be said to have a classical system of vocabulary. A wide variety of forms have developed out of this system in both music and dance. The more thoroughly a dancer is exposed to classical Form, both in music and dance, the greater the range of possibilities for the creation of new and exciting forms.

Historically, the development of music and dance have greatly affected one another; many forms of music were written specifically for the dance. At the time when court dancing flourished, Classical Ballet began to be created. Although at one time only certain styles of music were considered suited to the dance, today dances are choreographed to many styles of music from baroque and chamber music to symphonies and rock music. The only requirement is that the dance remain true to the nature of the music.

In primitive tribal dances, the human voice often accompanied the dancing. As finer qualities of instruments were developed, bringing more variety of sounds, the human voice was surpassed. New sounds were created that transcended imitations of nature's sounds. Musical instruments, however, are far from being foreign objects for human beings. They are an expression of a human need for the transcendent. The affinity we have for the sound and feel of a musical instrument transforms it into an expression of ourselves. In the same way, dancers absorb the sound of music into the instrument of their own bodies. The movement of the music becomes the movement of the dance.

The classical system of dance was developing in the courts of France and Italy in the late eighteenth and nineteenth centuries. The style was appropriately gentile, regal, elegant, elaborate, and formal.

33

The collaboration of artists was a primary ingredient in theatrical productions. In the seventeenth century, the brilliant Italian composer, Giovanni Baptiste Lully, saw that "coherence was the key to creation, and he insisted on having one librettist or poet, one composer, and only one designer working on any single presentation".[3] Lully's ideal can be seen in the collaboration of artists in present day choreographies in which art forms are integrated into coherent and lavish theatre and opera productions. Here are the early roots of our American musical and light opera.

In its traditional choreographies, the Classical Ballet retains the essential qualities originally conceived and developed out of European court dancing. As a result, dancers today are formally schooled in the structured training of posture, gesture, line, and quality of movement. The style definitely resembles the grand posture of an earlier day. Today the choreographer, who may re-design traditional works, must retain the style and intention of the original choreographer. Contemporary ballets can be choreographed in the classical style as well. The musical form chosen from the extensive repertory of classical music determines how the rules of the classical vocabulary are applied to the dance.

Many elements are combined to create forms of music. Silvano Arieti describes them as follows:

> Melody, one of the two essential components of music, has never lost its original function as expresser of emotion . . . The "breathing" of melody approximates some of the physiological concomitants of emotion . . . Rhythm, the other essential component of music, includes not only pulse and meter but also all the varieties of rhythmic groupings.[4]

These two basic components remind us of our primordial roots. They are responsible for the universal appeal the music shares with dance. Arieti continues,

> Harmony . . . is not nearly as ancient as melody and rhythm . . . as the simultaneous sounding of many different tones . . . [harmony] provides a textural element in music.

34

> Timber, which includes the concepts of tone-color and sonority in general, is defined as "the characteristic quality of sound". In music, timber is the chief supplier of aural pleasure. Metaphorically expressed, the timber-sensitive ear "feels" the quality of sound. These four components, originating at different levels of the psyche, are fused by form into the mode of creativity which is music.[5]

Through these four components of music we can arrive at a better understanding of classical form in dance The emotional content for a ballet traditionally is established through the melody of the music. The process of creatively constructing appropriate movements for a piece of music begins here. What does the emotional quality, expressed in the melody of the music, arouse in the choreographer? How is this emotion captured in classical movement? How does the pulse, the meter, and the basic rhythm relate to appropriate classical vocabulary? What is the texture of the music found in the harmony? How is the 'color' of the sound evident in its timber? For a classical ballet, the style of the movement will be limited by the traditional classical structure of the music. It will follow the form, and express the qualities of color, texture, rhythm, and emotional content inherent in the music, remaining precisely within the limits of the classical vocabulary of movements. Traditionally, the music for story ballets has been written specifically to meet the needs of both the story content and the classical dance vocabulary. The traditional ballet repertory includes many of these collaborations: *The Sleeping Beauty, Giselle, Coppelia* and *Swan Lake* are only a few. *Les Sylphides*, choreographed by Michel Fokine in 1909, was revolutionary in its time, for he chose an already composed collection of Chopin's music. The ballet simply expresses the quality and mood of the music in dance; it was choreographed in the romantic style using the classical technique. Eliminating a story and the ballerina as a technical star, it focused on the ensemble movement and musical quality.

Among choreographic innovators, Michel Fokine figures dramatically; as choreographer for the Ballets Russes, under the great impresario, Serge Diaghilev, he challenged the tradition of his time. The ballet had focused on the technical achievements of the dancers and fallen into a non-expressive exhibition of classical technique. Fokine's reformation re-established the "white ballet" of the romantic period by absorbing the classical technique into an expressive whole. Fokine said that the Dying Swan, "was proof that the dance could not, and should not, satisfy only the eye, but through the medium of the eye, should penetrate into the soul."[6]

At that moment, a new young choreographer came into the ballet world. Following Fokine as the next great genius and innovator of the Classical Ballet, George Balanchine has left us a legacy of one hundred and fifty ballets. He brings us from Europe to America. His Ballets stand as a magnificent tribute to the tradition established by Petipa. The innovative reforms of Fokine were brought to their most convincing extreme. Balanchine saw the Classical Ballet as purely and simply, "visual music". Before continuing the history of the development of ballet, we can gain insight into traditional dance and music by exploring in more detail what makes art "traditional".

8

Traditional Art

During the development of Western civilization a secularization of the arts took place: a shift from the religious to the romantic. Art became an expression of the human without conscious recognition of the divine or sacred. Seyyed Hossein Nasr explains that, "the Renaissance marked the beginning of the process of the radical secularization of man and knowledge, resulting in the humanism which characterizes this epoch."[1] In terms of dance, the Renaissance period was an era of creative growth, producing an aristocratic entertainment in the European courts. The themes of the dances were light and remote from life. After a surge of technical development, when teaching became stilted and dogmatic, the ballet became a middle class entertainment. With the undercurrents of the dawning seventeenth century—Age of Enlightenment or rationalism—Noverre brought a realistic element back into the Ballet. Then came the romantic eighteen hundreds. The influence of the Romantic Era remains in the Classical Ballet repertory to this day. By the end of the nineteenth century, another period of technical development produced the "glorification of the ballerina, virtuoso technique, the empty gesture of standardized beauty."[2]

The desacrilization of Western civilization has had its effect in every facet of modern living, from our science and language, to our philosophy and religion. Nasr identifies this as a loss of the

> unifying vision which related knowledge to love and faith, religion to science, and theology to all departments of intellectual concern . . . leaving a world of compartmentalization where there is no wholeness because holiness has ceased to be of central concern.[3]

I define sacred as the revelation of the Divine. It points toward the direction of the eternal and immutable reality. Nasr sees religion as that which binds human beings to God and lies at the heart of tradition. Secularization is a tendency to remove what is sacred from all human endeavors. The rediscovery of the sacred dimension in life explains this understanding of tradition. According to Nasr,

> Tradition, like religion, is at once truth and presence. It concerns the subject which knows and the object which is known. It comes from the Source from which everything originates and to which everything returns . . . Tradition is inextricably related to revelation and religion; to the sacred, to the notion of orthodoxy, to authority, to the continuity and regularity of transmission of the truth, to the exoteric and esoteric as well as to the spiritual life, science and the arts. The colors and nuances of its meaning become in fact clearer once its relation to each of these—is elucidated.[4]

To take the sacredness out of an art form is to remove the very essence of its tradition. This understanding of tradition evolves from a religious perspective. At the heart of every religion is a sense of perennial, or eternal, wisdom. In its truest sense, we can not speak of tradition without recognizing the religiousness, or sacredness of its definition. In Islamic writings, Nasr informs us that:

> true knowledge is identified with perennial wisdom which has existed since the beginning of human history. The Islamic

> conception of the universality of revelation went hand in hand with the idea of a primordial truth which has always existed, and will always exist, a truth without history. . . The term tradition is inseparable from the idea of permanent and perpetual wisdom.[5]

Religion binds humanity to God and to one another. Revelation is Logos, the word, or wisdom of God. It is God's means of revealing Himself to human beings. This perennial wisdom is the Primordial Tradition, or Origin of human existence, revealing Itself. It is "confirmed by each tradition through its doctrines and symbols, but also through the preservation of a 'presence' which is inseparable from the sacred."[6] From this perspective, each tradition stands as a revelation of truth that originates from the divine. It is passed down historically from generation to generation. "Man's sense of the sacred is none other than his sense for the Immutable and the Eternal, his nostalgia for what he really is, for he carries the sacred within the substance of his own being. . ."[7]

It is interesting to consider whether it is, in fact, possible to remove the sacred from any art form or any human search for knowledge. As theomorphic creatures, we need to be reminded of the nature of our being. Can we separate "knowing" from "being"? Or, "knowledge" from the "sacred"? In dance the roots of our heritage lie in this primordial sense of Tradition.

Our history of the Classical Ballet reveals a battle that continues to rage between the natural and the contrived. The great transitions in human history are quite precisely reflected in our art forms. Artists struggle with the current spirit of the times to maintain the integrity of art. This integrity is an expression of our deepest inheritance as human beings. The religious perspective of traditions allows an insight into the essence of the battle for integrity in dance. Art forms as traditions are seen from this perspective to be manifestations of the Primordial Tradition. All human knowledge is seen as evidence of divine presence. This movement of eternal and immutable reality is at once the Source of creation, and creation itself. The Classical in both music and dance far surpasses its own form, style, and system. It lays the ground for transforming innovation. It allows us to "see" the sacred movement at the heart of all traditions.

9

The Turning Point: The Twentieth Century

Historically, the twentieth century brings us to a turning point in dance. In nature, a balance must always be reached between extreme movements of life. The spirit of the Age of Reason and the industrial revolution overtook the mind of the eighteenth century. Our Classical Ballet artists flew to the rescue of the human "soul". They escaped into the romantic ballets of nymphs and spirits. Anything was preferable to the realism and concretism of a growing materialistic society. By the end of the nineteenth century the "romantic ideals of the Ballet had become classical spectacles with romantic overtones."[1]

The prominent choreographer of the period was Marius Petipa. He saw dance as a virtuoso spectacle of bravura classical technique. In spite of his understanding of technique and virtuosity, he has left us the epitome of romance in the *pas de deux* from such famous works as *The Sleeping Beauty, The Nutcracker,* and *Swan Lake.* Petipa's long reign, and responsibility for a tremendous evolution in the development of the Classical Ballet ended as a new balance was once again called for by the spirit of a new age and the advent of the twentieth century. A unique American woman gave birth to

41

what we now continue to call "modern" dance. Ballet had not yet "arrived" in America. While it flourished in Europe, Isadora Duncan virtually erupted into the world of dance. Her solo dances, unencumbered by classical costumes and *pointe* shoes, were totally spontaneous. They beautifully reflected her vision of dance as life— or religion.

> She gave the human body its natural rights. She delivered the dance from the fetters of mere entertainment and recreated the art in its oldest form: as a means to self-expression. She gave the twentieth century dancer his passport to freedom.[2]

Her influence on Michel Fokine, when he saw her dance in Russia, was to bring about a revolution in the Classical Ballet as well. In Germany the seeds were sown in Mary Wigman, another pioneer of modern dance. Her influence and schooling were transported to America by her pupil, Hanya Holm.[3] Modern dance has profoundly affected the Classical Ballet. It was as if the new age of "materialistic" society had to be re-vitalized by its own individualism. We had to reclaim our right to be self-expressive and freely innovative in order to move ahead into our contemporary nuclear age.

In an effort to bring Russian art to the world, the renowned impresario, Serge Diaghilev brought the Classical Ballet along with it. His vision made the reforms of Fokine possible. He established the Ballets Russes in Paris in 1909. It was founded on the premise of a profound understanding of the integration of music, painting, and dance. This collaboration of artists included the dancers, Nijinsky, Pavlova, and Karsavina; Fokine and Balanchine were two of the choreographers. The composers, Stravinsky and Prokofiev, joined the artists who designed the costumes and decors. As a result, the Classical Ballet began to gain world recognition. Artists like Pavlova toured the continents. The finest teachers of Classical Ballet settled everywhere in Europe and England. The relationship of classical music and ballet had been well established by the collaboration of artists such as Tchaikowsky and Petipa in Russia. With Diaghilev a collaboration was born that brings us to America with Igor Stravinsky and George Balanchine.

42

II

The Experience of Dance

In the last analysis, the essential thing is the life of the individual. This alone makes history, here alone do the great transformations first take place, and the whole future, the whole history of the world, ultimately spring as a gigantic summation from these hidden sources in individuals. In our most private and most subjective lives we are not only the passive witnesses of our age, and its sufferers, but also its makers.

C. G. Jung

10

Ballet in America

Balanchine points to the Russian Ballet for early signs of revolutionary development in the Classical Ballet. Under the direction of Petipa, Lev Ivanov choreographed the first two acts of *Swan Lake*, after the death of its composer, Tchaikovsky. Balanchine writes,

> Ivanov's two acts of *Swan Lake* have been an inspiration to many contemporary choreographers whose origin was pre-revolutionary Russia. If one man can be considered the pre-cursor of modern ballet, especially in the musical approach to choreography, that man was Lev Ivanov.[1]

In colonial America, social dancing thrived as it had in aristocratic European circles. Folk dances inherited from Europe inspired an American variety in the form of square dancing. Vaudeville, and the famous minstrel shows, became a popular form of entertainment. They provided an outlet for theatrical forms of dance. Visiting performers and companies toured America, including Anna Pavlova and the Ballets Russes, but it remained a European entity. By the beginning of the twentieth century the Classical Ballet had pervaded the cultural life of England and the Continent. Prominent academies were established in Denmark, Austria, France, Italy, and Russia. During this time, only an occasional unusually talented American ballet dancer emerged. After the death of Serge Diaghilev in 1929, the Ballets Russes dispersed. A company of some of the remaining dancers was formed under the name of the Ballet Russe de Monte Carlo. It began a series of many tours to America in 1933. At the same time, a School of American Ballet was being formed by Lincoln Kirstein and Edward Warburg with George Balanchine as the artistic director. An active dance community was forming in America. American choreographers, speaking the language of a pioneering country, developed a new vocabulary to express "America" in ballet. Included were Agnes de Mille's *Rodeo* and *Fall River Legend*, Eugene Loring's *Billy the Kid*, and Jerome Robbins' *Fancy Free*. Some of these works, along with many new American ballets remain in the repertory of American Ballet Theatre, founded in 1940 by Richard Pleasant and Lucia Chase. Balanchine's School of American Ballet, whose first performance was in 1934, continues to train dancers for the New York City Ballet. Through Balanchine, the Russian tradition flourished. Sorell writes that Balanchine had

> one foot in the nineteenth century, upholding the classical ballet tradition, as is plain in many of his works. And he considered himself the heir to Petipa's legacy. But, strangely enough, he also was attuned to the angularity and dissonance of our time. . . to respond quickly to the special gifts of American dancers and to the special cultural climate he found in the New World. . . The "Balanchine dancer" has become a trademark in the Ballet world.[2]

Balanchine's vision of the Classical Ballet was suited to what he perceived of American culture. He saw dance as "visual music". His long association with the composer, Igor Stravinsky, exemplified his belief in the tradition of a collaboration of composer and choreographer. He said,

> It is not an accident that dance masterpieces of Saint-Leon, Petipa, and Fokine all have scores that are also master works. Coppelia, the Sleeping Beauty, and Petroushka, with scores by Delibes, Tchaikovsky, and Stravinsky suggested to each of these choreographers an advance in the development of Ballet.[3]

He felt that the ballet was a complement to the sound of the music. Ballet could help the audience to appreciate the structure of the music by making the structure "visible". Balanchine and Stravinsky were two artists who reflected the vision of one another. Sorell describes Stravinsky's music as:

> theatrically intense, rhythmically insistent, reaching far back into "unashamed primitivism", dissonant, with a "sound of immediacy", full of surprises, and always pure. Balanchine responded to the vitality in the music; he learned to be guided by Stravinsky's dynamic use of silence; he accepted the constant surprise of his new approaches . . . He had the ability to grasp and express the meaning of the music.[4]

Balanchine felt that the meaning of the dance was not to be found in facial expressions or mannerisms but within the context of the whole bodily movement. Movement was the expression of the meaning of the music. He saw America as machines, technology, and experiment with the new. That vision was reflected in an abundance of experimental choreography. It also explains his expanded technical demands on the dancers. He looked for speed, precision, and flexibility. He personified American life through the dance. Balanchine described dance as a "woman". He dedicated his art to her. "Ballet is not intellectual, it's visual," he said. "Ballet has to be seen. It's like a beautiful flower. What can you say about a beautiful flower? All you can say is that it is beautiful."[5]

47

11

In Search of a Soul

The Russian Classical Ballet had as much effect on America as America had on it. With Balanchine's innovation, a classical American dancer emerged out of the classical tradition. There was a re-vitalization and reformation in dance that reflected the new America. It was a response to the time in history. Some of the most ancient precepts of dance were re-established. Marilyn Ferguson explains how dance, in the late nineteenth century, was left with a distorted sense of the Romantic period. She writes,

> The original meaning of Romance referred to the infinite and unfathomable, those forces in nature which are ever forming. Although it preferred the natural to the mechanistic, the Romantic movement was by no means anti-intellectual or anti-rational. Ironically, in their eagerness to probe the mysteries of nature, the Romantic period generated the scientific curiosity that finally led to the glorification of reason. Romance was then reduced to a cosmetic and trivial role, representing what is unreal, the gilt that hides the tarnish of life . . . in its heyday the Romantic movement celebrated family, friendship, nature,

art, music, literature, drawing on what one historian called "The mystery of the spirit, the larger self, the sense of quest." In a very real sense romance was identical with what we now call the spiritual. It trusted direct experience; it sought meaning.[1]

The struggle of our pioneers in American dance was valiant. They saw that our American values of freedom. independence, and human rights were part and parcel of what would bring the dance out of the realm of romantic trivia.

We cannot say that Isadora Duncan, and her modern dance contemporaries, were expressing a new reality in human experience. Rather, they renewed the original meaning of the Romantic period. Their experiments with movement gave expression to a quest for meaning. Influenced by Isadora, Fokine's reforms in the use of the classical vocabulary also reflected his quest for meaning. Balanchine carried Fokine's innovations to their most logical extreme. He found the meaning of dance in the structure of the music.

Innovators in modern dance saw the classical tradition as inconsequential to their quest. Yet Isadora, who blatantly recreated her innermost feelings in her improvisations, was the spark that inflamed Fokine's reforms in the classical idiom. Ruth St. Denis, turning to Eastern art and philosophy for her expression, discovered a call to become a "crusader for the sacred dance, creating, what she called, a 'rhythmic choir'."[2] Believing in the religious message of dance, she felt

that our civilization was growing decadent because "too many of us take from without instead of giving from within". . . . With the bible in her hands and a philosophy in her heart, she roamed far and wide in one-night stands with her orientalized dances and her faith in the holiness of the unity of body and soul.[3]

After World War II there was a movement toward sacred dance, or liturgical dancing, that was primarily inspired by Ruth St. Denis.

She and Ted Shawn formed the Denishawn School which was to mark the beginning of modern dance in America. Having begun his education as a student of Theology, his call to dance was to "preach a sermon, not with words, but with every fiber of the body."[4] As a result, the Denishawn School launched a spiritual revolution in modern dance. Those in search of a personal dance expression, indicative of their own time, left to explore and create. Among them were the pioneers of American modern dance, Martha Graham, Doris Humphrey, Louis Horst, and Charles Weidman.

Modern dancers were not only reflecting a need of the times, they were searching for a "soul" that belongs to the dance. Reflecting the pioneer spirit of America, they pioneered the way to a freedom of expression that enters the lives of all who dwell in America. The modern dance, the American musical, and jazz in music and dance are our national art forms. They express the spirit of American life. Touching the hearts of us all, they have become our American heritage. This search for expression is as personal and unique as it is universal. For St. Denis and Shawn, the message was sacred. For many of those modern dancers who followed, the message was taken from the bible and mythology. These became an avenue to the expressive soul of dance. De Mille, Loring and Robbins brought the pioneering spirit into the American Ballet Theatre repertory. Balanchine saw the American dancer as the epitome of his "approach to pure ballet, in which the moving body alone must create artistic excitement and evoke images of fantasy and human relationships."[5]

Suzanne K. Langer concludes that plastic art, pantomime, or visual music describes the material that makes up the elements of the dance. She sees dance as an independent art form: as rhythmic motion transformed into gesture. She writes:

> The gesture becomes a symbolic movement in the imagination of the choreographer who makes use of it to express his ideas of different feelings . . . dance, independent of music, sculpture, painting, pantomime, or drama has an energy and life of its own.[6]

Both modern and classical ballet choreographers have experimented with dances created in silence. They play upon intuitive body rhythms, spatial patterns, and the powerful energy of relationship felt among the dancers. We speak of dance in terms of powerful forces and individually created energies and tensions. Dance produces a spontaneous source of vitality that empowers the whole piece with an energy and life of its own. Choreographic genius gives birth to new life. The mood, atmosphere, emotion, and quality of the assembled whole surpasses the sum of the individuals. The energy created as a result, of the interconnection of energies, breathes something original into life. It miraculously grows, changes, and flows differently with each performance; no two performances of a dance are the same. This is the challenge of the performing arts. It makes dance a truly living art form. In searching for a soul, dancers find the soul of dance. Dance takes its rightful place as an expression of the real sense of Romance. It is a quest for meaning. Modern dancers returned to religious themes and inner emotional experiences. Thus, they recalled the original sacredness of dance that belongs to its primitive ritualistic tradition. The soul of dance lives in the heart of its own tradition. It reflects the Tradition from which all traditions are born.

12

Creativity

There is a wealth of literature that explores the process of creativity in human beings. The mysterious nature of creativity raises questions in every area of human activity. All categories of science and liberal arts have sought explanations. Human creativity is a phenomenon that both eludes and intrigues us.

Because we respond to both the arts and religion as a calling, we tend to see them as vocations, rather than professions. Marilyn Ferguson suggests that

> vocation has more the quality of an inner summons to move in a particular direction, feeling one's way, or of a vision, a glimpse of the future that is more preview than plan. A vision can be realized in many ways, a goal, only in one...The individual with a vocation finds meaningful work. A vocation is not a job. It is an on-going transformative relationship.[1]

Our great innovators in dance have found their work to be profoundly meaningful. The transformation of primitive ritualistic dancing into an evolving modern art form suggests a transforming relationship between dancers and their art form. The relationship is interdependent. The effect of transformation is equally visible in the growing, changing artist as it is in the developing, maturing art form. This is the transforming effect of the creative process itself. It also indicates that an exploration of creativity from the psychological perspective must have at least two approaches. According to Carl Jung,

> The task of psychology in relation to the arts might be to explain the process of creativity in producing a work of art, and on the other hand to explore the factors that make a person artistically creative.[2]

Jung has much to say about the vocation of an artist:

> Art is a kind of innate drive that seizes a human being and makes him its instrument. The artist is not a person endowed with free will who seeks his own ends, but one who allows art to realize its purposes through him. As a human being he may have moods and a will and personal aims, but as an artist he is "man" in a higher sense...he is collective man...one who carries and shapes the unconscious and psychic life of mankind...Every creative person is a duality or a synthesis of contradictory aptitudes. On the one side he is a human being with a personal life, while on the other he is an impersonal creative process...The specifically artistic disposition involves an over-weight of collective psychic life as against the personal...it is sometimes necessary for him to sacrifice happiness and everything that makes life worth living for the ordinary human being...[His] ruthless passion for creation may go so far as to override every personal desire...There are hardly any exceptions to the rule that a person must pay dearly for the divine gift of the creative fire. How can we doubt that it is his art that explains the artist, and not the insufficiencies and conflicts of his personal life? The work in process becomes the poet's fate and determines his psychic development. It is not Goethe who creates Faust, but Faust which creates Goethe.[3]

Karen Horney, another psychoanalyst of the early twentieth century, discusses a long disputed relationship of art and neurosis. She stands against those psychologists who suggest that inner conflict and tension and external conflicts are a cause, and even a necessary pre-requisite, for creative activity. Horney proposes that, "an artist creates despite his neurosis, not because of it."[4] In her understanding, all human beings have within them a vital life force of energy impelling them toward self-realization. This "real self" is the essential aspect of the creating self. "The less self-conscious, the less intimidated, the less a person tries to comply with expectations of others, the less the need to be right or perfect, the better he can express whatever gifts he has."[5] She disputes the idea that inner tension is necessary for creative activity. Life itself has sufficient real tension without neurotic conflicts. She says, "This is particularly true for an artist, with his greater than average sensitivity to beauty and harmony but also to discords and suffering, and with his greater capacity for emotional experience."[6]

Jung describes two different "modes of creation":

> In one the artist subordinates the material to his own artistic purposes. The artist is so identified with his work that his intentions and his faculties are indistinguishable from the act of creation itself. . . [In the other, the artist is] overwhelmed by a flood of thoughts and images which he never intended to create and which his own will could never have brought into being. . . his work is greater than himself and wields a power which is not his and which he cannot command. Here the artist is not identical with the process of creation; he is aware that he is subordinate to his work or stands outside of it.[7]

He also believed that

> The personal idiosyncracies that creep into a work of art are not essential: in fact, the more we have to cope with these pecularities, the less it is a question of art. What is essential in a work of art is that it should rise far above the realm of personal life and speak from the spirit and heart of the poet as man to the spirit and heart of mankind.[8]

Jung concludes that creativity in human beings remains, and perhaps will remain forever, within the realm of the mysterious.

Silvano Arieti explores a theory of primary, secondary, and tertiary modes of operation in human cognition in which he describes a "magic synthesis". In the third mode of operation, creative persons see a way of bringing about the "magic synthesis" that produces a newness. They envision totality or unity. Arieti suggests a kind of linear ascent, or evolutionary process, in the study of creativity itself. He envisions human beings opening to increasingly vast horizons as they add dimensions to their climb. In the final analysis, however, "the creative person remains the keeper of the secret of what makes his personality creative. . .a secret that he cannot reveal to himself or to others."[9] The dance itself is a means of exploring human creativity. It allows the mysterious ascent to unfold before us. In a sense, the choreographed work personifies the process of creativity or the magic synthesis. The experience of dance is a creative process that insists that we strive to reach for connection: to one another, and to all creation.

Isadora believed that dance is life. Martha Graham sought to free the American spirit through her exploration of human nature. Ruth St. Denis sought to express the unity of body and soul revealing the sacredness of dance. Robbins, Loring, and de Mille brought forth the legends of pioneer America. Balanchine saw the epitome of dance as "visual music", in the American dancer. We conclude with Arieti's description of creative man:

> Although he will not reach the peak of the ultimate mountain, the horizons that open before his eyes are vaster and vaster. And he rejoices in his heart, knowing that his labor has not been in vain, since those horizons will be shared by millions of brothers and sisters, not just today, but as long as people will live on earth. Thus, what remained unfinished as a cognitive ascent, finds an end in an act of social love.[10]

13

The Craft

In our eagerness to explain and understand the mysteries of human growth and creativity, even our most diligent explorers are drawn to a kind of reductionism in the joy of a new found theory. It seems to grasp the whole truth when, in reality, it remains only a small clue. It is still another pointer in the direction we must travel. Thus far, I have attempted to lay the ground historically, psychologically, and spiritually to prepare for an exploration into the realm of possibility and imagination. To enter this vast arena of creative adventure, we turn to those who can lead the way.

The growth and development of the Classical Ballet is dependent on a collaboration of innovative choreographers and talented dancers. The composer, playwright, and choreographer need performers for their work. All of them require an audience. The effectiveness of dance depends upon the energy that creates connections between the choreographer, dancers, musicians and audience. On this level, all the connections and energies meet on common ground.

The early innovators of modern dance were each unique as

creative performers. They were primarily solo performing artists. Experimenting with their own personal vision of dance, they used their own bodies as expressive instruments. When a school, or style of expressive movement, developed, it was often years later. Here the innovative choreographer and the performing artist were the same person. In the Classical Ballet, the great innovators were often excellent performers. However, their genius lay in the vision they had of the potential inherent in the Classical Ballet as a school. They made use of the system, style, and technique as a mode of dance expression. Their innovations were the result of personal experience with the Classical Ballet tradition. Their personal charism as performers was not essential to their creativity in dance. The challenge is great for both ballet and modern dance choreographers when using a company of dancers. It is comparable to a composer hearing his musical compositions played by a variety of musicians or orchestras. It is a unique experience in dance. The dancers are asked to feel, and express with their bodies, the personal sensitivity and vision of the choreographer. The craft includes an ability to sense the innate talent and technical capabilities of individual dancers. Utilizing them to the maximum can produce a vital choreographic effect. Choreographers often design works that are inspired by the talented dancers standing before them. Balanchine stressed the individuality of his dancers and encouraged their unique potential. For this reason, dancers found themselves discovering who they were in an exciting collaboration. In a sense, this is contrary to the European tradition of classical ballet where the corps de ballet is a unified ensemble. It must move with as closely identical lines as possible. Only the soloists and an especially chosen few become the exceptions. In a good corps de ballet, all the dancers create the illusion of being the same. Thus, the individuality of the ballerina or solo male dancer is all the more noticeable. It is a striking paradox, and tribute to Balanchine's genius, that his dancers were identified as "Balanchine dancers", yet were encouraged to discover their unique potential.

The craft of choreography is not comparable to other fields where there is a well recorded method of learning the skill. Like the ballet technique itself, choreographies pass from generation to generation through the memories of the dancers, teachers, and choreographers themselves. Young choreographers learn by imitating what has been done before. They can also break from tradition into personal choreographic expressions.[1] We know that notation and recording methods are necessary for art forms to preserve their traditions. Advanced technology has benefitted the dance. Video and films help to alleviate the difficulty in preserving the great masterpieces of the dance.

Balanchine writes,

> A choreographer must see things that other people don't notice, to cultivate his visual sense. . . He must know music. . . know how to play it, preferably, and how to read it. . . The structure of a ballet must be tight, compact, like the structure of a building; good ballets move in measured space and time, like the planets. . . The choreographer frees his mind from the limitations of practical time in much the same way that the dancer has freed his body. He turns not away from life, but to its source. He uses his technical proficiency to express in movement his essential knowledge. Talent, inspiration, and personality are not sources which come to an artist in a flash and go away: they are the accumulated results of all he has felt, thought, seen and done. . . the stories he heard as a child, the art he has enjoyed, his education, and his everyday life. . . and are always with him, capable of being reached by his technical ability and transformed into dynamic designs of the utmost intensity.[2]

There are many aspects of creative human perception that have contributed to the craft as we experience it in the dance today.

14

Symbol and Image

The human capacity for play is a contributing factor in our creative activity. Animals have no ability to play with forms and sounds in the way that human beings can. By our ability to play, we are drawn to create new stimuli for ourselves. We play with forms, images, and ideas that not only communicate thoughts and feelings, but also effectively create an impact "of the utmost intensity". Our ability to play with forms, symbols, shapes, images, and ideas contributes extensively to our understanding of the creative process.

Carl Jung suggests that one source of creativity is the intrusion of unconscious material into the conscious mind of the artist. He explored the primordial images behind the imagery of art. A work of art, he said, "as well as being symbolic, has its source, not in the personal unconscious of the poet, but in a sphere of unconscious mythology whose primordial images are the common heritage of mankind."[1] Jung called these primordial images archetypes. They correspond to Plato's universal Ideas, or Forms. Huston Smith comments on Jung's treatment of the archetypes:

"dreams coincide to such a degree with the world's mythologies...that the symbols themselves must reside in man's collective unconscious." They have an energy of their own, sufficient to have caused Jung to regard them as the psychic counterparts of biological instincts. Physically man's life is vectored by his biological drives; psychically it is molded by the surging pressure of the archetypes.[2]

In his studies Jung found:

> The primordial image, or archetype, is a figure—be it a demon, a human being, or a process—that constantly recurs in the course of history and appears wherever creative fantasy is freely expressed. Essentially, therefore, it is a mythological figure...They give form to countless experiences of our ancestors...In each of these images there is a little piece of human psychology and human fate, a remnant of the joys and sorrows that have been repeated countless times in our ancestral history, and on the average follow ever the same course.[3]

The craft of choreography contains an enormous range of possibilities. Rich resources of music are available, and a comparable range of movement potential. But the craft invites us to explore the art. Proceeding into the realm of symbol, image, and myth, the art of choreography suggests creativity and human imagination.

Imagination is a pre-requisite for creative activity. Silvano Arieti describes imagination as

> the capacity of the mind to produce or reproduce several symbolic functions while in a state of conciousness, or awakeness, without any effort to organize these functions...Imagery is only one type of imagination; it is the process of producing and experiencing images.[4]

"A symbol is a representative of something else, even when that 'something else' is completely absent."[5] writes Arieti. The words that make up our language systems are our most common symbols. They convey images which express ideas or feelings symbolically. The development of languages is a sign of the historical cultural growth of civilizations. However, the process of communication through word symbols has limitations that are easily seen when we try to express some of our most human emotional experiences. Suddenly, gestures, facial expressions, and other forms of movement are necessary to communicate beyond the written or spoken word. We are trying to communicate on a deeper, more lasting level where words fail us. We are reminded of de Mille's definition of art. Our capacity as human beings to play with symbols, in new and different ways, is also a basis of creativity.

We said that our ability to produce and experience images is a type of imagination. Psychologically it is considered to be a primary thought process. Images are an important means of establishing an inner sense of reality. We can visually image the persons and places of our daily experience which allows us to recall them at will, and absorb them into becoming a part of who we are. There are two important types of images, the visual and the auditory. Both are essential components of the creative process in the art of choreography. A mental image can be a representation of some subjective, real experience. It can recall all the feelings and emotions associated with that experience. The image is not identical to the original perception, therefore, it can be a means to the mental creation of something new. Images also tend to lead us to other associations or remind us of other visual images. The development of a visual imagination is crucial for choreography. It makes use of the craft and artistic form. It also allows the choreographer to visualize a sequence of ballet steps in a new , expanded, or altered way. They may become a representation of something else or a symbol. Choreographers freely associate movements in their imagination. Apparently human beings have varied abilities to produce images. I suggest that artists have tremendously developed capacities— particularly dancers and choreographers. The choreographer visualizes movement and conveys it to the dancers. They, in turn, physically reproduce the perception. Dancers retain hundreds of ballets in their memories: visualizing every movement, quality of expression, and tiny nuance of style, rhythm, timing, and spatial patterns is a means of mentally "rehearsing" before performances.

The auditory image seems to be less common for most people, yet dancers and choreographers have a kind of "music memory" that is extremely well developed. Often in remembering ballets danced years before, the music is the means to total movement recall. For the choreographer, as Balanchine pointed out, the development of auditory images in relation to music is essential. The choreographer's ability to visualize movement and hear music in different ways, through visual and auditory image is part of the creative process in choreography.

Imaging is one way that human beings can reproduce reality. We can also alter it, expand upon it, or create a totally new image. This can be related to Jung's concept of the archetype or universal collection of primordial, mythological images. It also relates to his concept of the unconscious in relation to creativity. Apparently Jung felt that

> the creative process consists of an unconscious animation of the archetype. The primordial image, connected with the archetype, compensates for the insufficiency and onesidedness of the creative person's experience of life, or even of the spirit of the historical time in which the creative person lives . . . The artist's lack of adaptation to his environment becomes his real advantage; it facilitates the re-emergence of the archetype; it induces him to enter into a mystical participation with the ancient sources.[6]

In other words, Jung implies that the creative person is particularly sensitive to the messages he receives into his consciousness from the deeper psychological levels of his unconscious mind. He especially notes those images which arise out of the collective unconscious in recognizable, universally understandable, archetypal forms. That is what Jung suggests is responsible for the universal appeal of traditional art forms. Jung felt that we are all mysteriously bound to one another through ages of inherited human collective unconscious experiences. We are reminded that creativity must not be reduced to a simple formula. As religious philosopher, Huston Smith, points out,

> The mistake of reductionism—spirit reduced to metamorphosed matter (Darwinism), truth reduced to ideology (Marxism), psyche reduced to sex (Freud). . . lies in its attempt to explain the greater in terms of the less, with the not too surprising consequence that the greater is thereby lessened. It is this, at root, that sets us against the modern outlook and turns us back toward tradition where the drift is always the reverse: to explain the lesser by means of the more, a mode of explanation that tends to augment rather than deplete.[7]

The archetype is an ancient mythological representation of figures or images that point to universal human concepts. Reappearing in the mythologies, religions, rituals, and beliefs of societies throughout history, the archetype reveals itself in different forms despite the cultural, intellectual, and technological achievements, or sophistication of the society. Inevitably, they manifest themselves most poignantly in the realm of the artist but hardly exclusively. How we experience the archetype is determined by the psychology of each individual. Carried to its farthest extreme, Jung's theory implies that creativity in human beings can be reduced to a continual reemerging process of universal imagery. In effect, it reproduces itself over and over again in art forms as ever-new, yet ever-old manifestations of ancient truths. The theory seems to miss the awesome experience of great art, and the particular genius that can surprise us with something new. Are we simply varied reproductions of earlier members of the species? Or are we mysteriously, and wonderfully, unique creations? Jung himself was inclined to admit the mysteriousness of great art, and the elusive aspects of creativity in individuals. From a religious perspective, isn't God so enraptured with Being, that He cannot resist any of its possibilities? Nevertheless, Jung's insights on creativity spark our interest in primordial images, collective unconscious archetypes, and mythological figures. How have they affected, or continue to affect our classical and modern forms of dance?

One of the foremost innovators of modern dance dramatically reveals image and symbol in dance. Martha Graham felt that her body was meant to give physical form to her beliefs. "Like a prophet, or messiah, she felt compelled to dance the truth as she saw it."[8] Her dances gave expression to the universal and timeless experiences of humanity. She created ritual dances out of her belief in the need of humanity for ritual. She took the quality of human emotions from their deepest level, as meaningful expressions of universal human experience, and made them visible in bodily movement. The names of her early works describes their contents very well. They include, *Two Primitive Canticles, Primitive Mysteries, Ceremonials*, and the famous *Lamentation*. Walter Terry describes *Lamentation*:

> Here was a figure contracted in agony, seeking unconsciously the safe position of the fetus, pulled and twisted by visceral pains of anguish, letting the body rack itself in self-flagellation, pushing the feet into the floor, looking up to escape, or to God, shrouded in the confining fabric of sorrow. And each who saw this ritual of lamentation could apply it to himself and to his own experiences, for this was not a case history but, rather, an objectifying in physical form of the lamentations of all men.[9]

Here is the universal Idea, in the form of suffering and sorrow. The archetype of all human suffering and the powerful image of human tragedy lead us to another turning point. Comparative mythology provides a deeper dimension of the art of choreography through its universal symbols and images.

15

Myth

Joseph Campbell suggests that mythology is the mother of the arts. The ability of human beings to play with forms, symbols, ideas, and images is imbedded in the heart of mythology, just as it is in all art forms. The study of mythology involves an extensive exploration of human developmental processes. It gives rise to questions as to what is innate, conditioned, imprinted, or instinctual in human beings. Through mythology, we observe responses and stimulants with an eye to the historical, biological, sociological, and psychological effect on human development and behavior. As we shall see, mythology is intertwined with primordial, or archetypal, imagery. Mythical imagery surfaces from deep levels of the psyche into human creative activity. A study of mythology beckons us to return to the ritual of primitive societies and the development of religion. Religion is an expression of a human need to find order and meaning through ritual and myth. In *The Masks of God*, author Joseph Campbell explores Primitive, Oriental, Occidental, and Creative Mythology. He takes the figures and themes from their primitive roots and compares them to the themes that permeate our religions and arts to this day. The mythology of cultures, from the earliest known to the contemporary, probe into the most revealing aspects of the spiritual and philosophical realities of human societies. It is mythology that shapes our culture as much as it is our culture that shapes mythology. It determines our ritual and indicates our deepest religious convictions. A study of mythology impresses us with the extent of common experience shared by human societies.

Today, we commonly tend to dismiss everything that falls into the category of myth as something false, unreal, or imaginary, and therefore, simply a story that doesn't warrant serious attention. However, the heroes, heroines, and themes that appear in the stories of mythology are the universal symbols that provided the basis for Jung's understanding of the archetypes. They continue to surface in our dreams and fantasies. We cannot ignore them, for they will not be dismissed so easily. They surface despite us, finding their expression in our religions, folklore, literature, art, and even in games and politics. Often their true origin is not recognized. Mythological symbols are a factor in the universal appeal of great works of art. As Campbell points out, mythology awakens us to the wonder and mystery of the universe. It presents that mystery in the form of contemporary meaningful imagery. In the ritual and moral ordering of social groups, our mythology continues to provide a sense of well being and harmony, just as it did in primitive societies.

> The most critical function of a mythology is to foster the centering and unfolding of the individual in integrity, in accord with himself (the microcosm), his culture (the mesocosm), the universe (the macrocosm), and the awesome ultimate mystery which is both beyond and within himself and all things.[1]

Campbell explores traditional mythology in relation to his "Creative Mythology". To the extent that traditional mythologies become our cultural heritage, they tend to determine the experience and expression of individuals. However, Campbell notes that traditions begin as an expression of individual experience.

68

> . . . just as in the past each civilization was the vehicle of its
> own mythology, developing in character as its myth became
> progressively interpreted, analyzed, and elucidated by its
> leading minds, so in this modern world . . . where the applica-
> tion of science to the fields of practical life has now dissolved
> all cultural horizons, so that no separate civilization can ever
> develop again . . . each individual is the center of a mythology
> of his own intelligible character, is the Incarnate God, so to
> say, whom his empirically questing consciousness is to
> find . . . [This is] what I am here calling creative myth, which
> springs from the unpredictable, unprecedented experience in
> illumination of an object by a subject, and the labor then, of
> achieving communication of the effect. It is in this second,
> altogether secondary, phase of creative art, communication,
> that the general treasury, the dictionary so to say, of the world's
> rich heritage of symbols, images, myth motives, and hero
> deeds, may be called upon . . . either consciously, as by Joyce
> and Mann, or unconsciously, as in dream . . . to render the
> message.[2]

It appears that individual experience transforms universal
mythological themes.

The history of civilization indicates how human beings have
passed from primitive/collective societies into highly cognitive
individuals. In the process, we have discovered a sense of
personhood, and increasing levels of consciousness. Studies in
human growth and development indicate a maturation process in
individuals: we grow from finding meaning in our environment and
social milieu, into searching for identity and meaning within
ourselves. As we pass from one state of personal development
into the next, there is a time of transition. Our earlier years are
generally an adaptation to society and finding our place in the
external world. Then there is a transition leading us into the second
half of life: we begin an inner search for life's meaning. This is a
pattern reflected in the history of civilizations. It inevitably appears
in our art forms as well. In the dance, the twentieth century marked
a turning point—a transition through which we are still growing.

Transitions are a time of growth and change. In Western civilization, the beginning of the twentieth century encouraged individuality and self-conscious awareness. In our society, the authorities of past generations are questioned in all fields. The secular has overshadowed inherited religious values and institutions. Our individual integrity is tested by the extremes of a highly developed technological society. It is a time of transition, from separate cultures and civilizations into a whole-world cultural viewpoint. The artist remains the mediator and explorer into universal, timeless, and eternal truths. As Campbell suggests, those are the messages communicated through our rich heritage of human mythologies.

The ritual of primitive people was given expression and meaning through movement. We know that biblical people danced. Walter Sorell tells us that a sacred dance ritual was the source of the Catholic Mass for the early Christians. The myth or story form of a deep religious conviction was personified in a ritualistic dance. Ancient myths of all cultural origins—Greek, Egyptian, Oriental— have always sparked the imagination of our Western innovators of theatrical dance forms. They inspired the works of our twentieth century modern dancers from Isadora Duncan and Ruth St. Denis to Martha Graham. Their subjects ranged from Egyptian and Oriental theatrical pieces to the Greek Tragedies.

In the Classical Ballet we have many traditional ballets using themes from folklore: legendary heroes and heroines of many different national traditions have found their way to the ballet stage. Nor has the Classical Ballet been any less intrigued by the aura of mythological symbolism and the images that evoke that symbolism. Thus we find a sylph in *La Sylphide*, and nymphs in Fokine's *Les Sylphides*. The images of romantic, supernatural Wilis, in *Giselle*, along with the Swan Queen, make us wonder about the symbolism carried by the ballerina in these masterpieces of Classical Ballet history.

Balanchine describes the Ballet as "woman". We can discreetly venture into the Idea, or archetype, of this universal, mythological identity of the feminine. Here is the nymph, the eternally virginal Wilis, and the dual role of Odette/Odile, the white and black swan.

She is the universal Idea of the dualism of good and evil, barren and fertile, earth and heaven, that gives substance to the mythological image or archetype of female/woman. She is called many names by many traditions. She embodies the paradoxes of all of life, and of death. This Great Goddess of the universe is Queen Isis, Minerva, Diana, Venus and many others. She permeates the symbolic personifications of mother, earth, life, and the universe. She appears as the Hindu mother-goddess, Kali, who personifies life, or the universe, brings forth life only to devour it. And yet she is

> simultaneously the goddess Annapurna (meaning food and abundance), India's counterpart of the Egyptian Isis with the sun-child Horus at her breast, or of Babylonian Ishtar, nurs-ing the moon-god reborn, the archaic prefigurements in Mediterranean mythology and art of the Madonna of the Middle Ages.[3]

These primitive mythologies grew out of the mystery inherent in the world of nature. The primitive mystery surrounding lifebearing woman as the original mother has caused ages of humankind to seek relationship, co-operation and integration through its rites, rituals, and mythological stories, personifications, and symbols.

Campbell describes the perennial roles of our mother-goddess by referring to the Roman Catholic "Litany of Loredo", which is addressed to the Virgin Mother Mary. She is called: Holy Mother of God, Mother of Divine Grace, Mother of Good Counsel; Virgin most renowned, Virgin most powerful, Virgin most merciful, Virgin most faithful; she is praised as the Mirror of Justice, Seat of Wisdom, Cause of our Joy, Gate of Heaven, Morning Star, Health of the Sick, Refuge of Sinners, Comforter of the Afflicted, Queen of Peace, Tower of David, Tower of Ivory, and House of God.[4] She is called the Mother of Sorrows and Our Lady of Perpetual Help. The imagery is compelling. It is as pregnant as the Virgin herself with life and hidden meanings that pour forth infinite possibilities for meditation. They could easily give rise to equally infinite possibilities in corresponding symbolic movement. The symbol of Mother-

Goddess-Woman is related to still other deeply meaningful psychological symbols. The womb itself symbolizes a return to eternity. The amniotic fluid is a primary life substance responsible for the powerful symbol of water in mythology and Jungian psychology. The cycles of nature are equally mysterious symbols of new life, death, and rebirth. Symbolic female figures keep watch over the waters. These sea-nymphs, sirens, and ladies of the lake are either life-threatening or life-giving. We recognize our nymphs, maidens, and swan queens from the Classical Ballet repertory. They are easily related to these highly symbolic mythological personifications. The Mother-GoddessWoman, female archetype, appears in all mythologies from the primitive, through our traditional religions, to our contemporary art forms.

In turning to creative mythology, we find individual artists at the center of their own mythology. Perhaps it is that center which inspired the vision of Ballet as woman. The subject of creative mythology is rich with possibilities. It contains a wealth of imagery and inspiration. We can even say that there is an aura of myth that belongs to the Classical Ballet itself, as in the image of the "ballerina". She is the embodiment of all that is beautiful in women. As the perfection of the feminine, she is the Ideal, or symbol, of grace, finesse, warmth, and classical purity of movement. But she also embodies power, strength, beauty of form, and sculptural line. There are equally strong images of the male dancer. He personifies the hero, the perfect lover, the grand escort, and protector. In the traditional classical *pas de deux*, we have the personification of the Ideal of romantic love. Here is the true myth of eros in the synchronized movements of the two dancers. We see the power of the male dancer as he effortlessly lifts the seemingly weightless ballerina into the air and escorts her gallantly across the stage. The Classical Ballet is enveloped in a created living myth of its own, which is revealed in the art of choreography. It will continue to be created and re-created in the life of dance through the unique talent of its artists. The symbols, images, and mythological figures will appear in ever-new forms. They will also be miraculously transformed into a new variety of living myth. We see the world from where we are standing at any given moment. Our attitudes and experience give new dimensions to what we envision. Our contemporary choreographers will bring their mythologies to life through their art.

The perspective of mythology expands the dimensions of the art of dance. We are pointed toward the mystery that is hidden within our symbols, images, and myth. As we continue our journey into the heart of dance, mystery reveals itself and living myth is born. "Mythology is a rendition of forms through which the Form of forms can be known. An inferior object is presented as the re-presentation, or habitation, of a superior."[5]

16

The Vicarious Experience

In Part One of this study, we spoke of the movements of self-expression, relationship, and communication as essential to our sense of well-being as persons. Communication is a universal human desire. In psychological terms, it is a secondary thought process. It is the movement we make toward one another in our desire for communion. Communion is a gathering together to become one with others. We wish to speak to the heart of another, hoping to touch at the deepest level of our common humanity. I reveal to you who you are by revealing who I am.

Communications is a fast developing field of modern technology. Because communications skills are so vital to our evolving global civilization, it has become a priority in our society. Information televised via satellite for global accessibility allows us to know about world affairs within minutes of an actual event. We are in visual contact with world issues and with the people of nations. In an earlier age, they would have remained for most of us solely in the realm of our imagination, as distant, unknown, and foreign cultures. Thus, our need to communicate in terms of infor-

...ation is being met at more highly developed levels than ever before in history. Yet, at the intra-personal and inter-personal levels, we find ourselves in the midst of an identity crisis. We are deeply affected by the increasing depersonalization of our technological age. Individual and collective mental health, a sense of wellbeing, and personal purpose have become simultaneous global concerns. These are equally important issues for modern scientific research, growth, and development. Current literature suggests that the rate of change in every area of modern living is dangerously overwhelming. The ability of individuals to continually adapt to a rapidly changing environment is taking its toll in mental health. "Traditional", as an ability to stabilize living, and provide for individual and collective identity and meaning, has become an anachronism in our society. Religion, family, community, and nationality, as symbols of values and deeply significant commitments, are subject to question. It follows that the artist and traditional forms of art are subject to re-evaluation as well.

One of the intentions of great works of art is to create an impact whose nature relates to creativity and the process of communication. This kind of communication has subtleties, variations, and a depth of quality that deserves our attention. In Chapter Twelve, we quoted Carl Jung's description of two modes of artistic creativity. In the first, artists can intentionally create works of art in which they are so identified that the work becomes the natural expression of the artist's own personality. The second mode of creativity is beyond personal intention. The creative idea articulates itself through the medium of the artist. There are two corresponding ways to experience works of art. In one, the work of art is taken as complete in itself. All that is meant to be heard, felt, or discerned is clearly, and unmistakably, visible. Nothing is required of the receiver of the communication but to be present to the work. It speaks for itself, and its message is clearly evident in the artist's medium of expression. The second is seen as sending messages of a variety of deeply symbolic meanings, making use of the vast spectrum of symbol, image and myth. Here the receivers are provoked into their imaginations. They rely on elusive areas of individual

76

intuition and perception in order to grasp the diversity of messages. That diversity may or may not be intended by the artist.

Meerloo's essays on creativity as instinct, explore the relationship of the emotions expressed by the artist in the work of art and those received by the audience.[1] He explains that there is a tension in every form of communication, because of the need for harmony between the rhythms of one's own inner world and those of the outer world. The emotion expressed in a work of art (the outer world) must be integrated with those emotions being felt by the observer. The difference between the emotions being sent by the artist and those felt by the receiver is the source of tension in all forms of communication. He points out that even artists may receive different messages from their own work, depending on how they feel at the time. We tend to project our own inner reality into all that we experience. The variation in our experiencing inevitably colors how we experience the impact of works of art, as well. We can understand how works of art make an impact by seeing the relation of Jung's collective unconscious to creativity. He explains that we must be

> able to let a work of art act upon us as it acted upon the artist. To grasp its meaning, we must allow it to shape us as it shaped him. Then we can understand the nature of his experience. We see that he has drawn upon the healing and redeeming forces of the collective psyche that underlies consciousness with its isolation and painful errors; that he has penetrated to that matrix of life in which all men are imbedded, which imparts a common rhythm to all human existence, and allows the individual to communicate his feelings and his striving to mankind as a whole. The secret of artistic creation and of the effectiveness of art is to be found in a return to the state of "participation mystique". . . to that level of experience at which it is man who lives, and not the individual, and at which the weal and woe of the single human being does not count, but only human existence. That is why every great work of art is objective and impersonal, but none the less profoundly moves us each and all.[2]

We are touched by those elements in a work of art that are universal expressions of human experience. Whether we recognize the symbolism of a Swan Queen as a primitive mythological Mother Goddess makes no difference. We are brought to tears by the agonizing movements of *Lamentations*, and feel an uplifting sensation after an electrifying performance of a romantic *pas de deux*. We are taken immediately out of ourselves and deeply into our own inner reality by the mysterious mode of communication in great works of art.

In a world where the field of communications has been taken over by modern technology, are traditional art forms still meaningful? Do they reach our deepest human desire to be touched by, and to reach out to touch, the hearts and minds of others? A new mythology is being created by our artists in every traditional art form. Do they have the power to heal our identity crisis at the intra-personal and inter-personal levels?

We noted that much of what was once considered the established authority and known as traditional in our society has become an anachronism: it is considered out-of-tune with our historical times. I suggest that when any human way of perceiving becomes an anachronism it is an open invitation to change, to revolutionize, and to grow. Out of dying traditions, very alive innovations are born. That is what our mythologists, psychiatrists, and psychologists verify as the role of the artist in our society. Artists translate traditional art forms into relevant contemporary language. They continue to point the way back to and forward toward what has always been Traditional through the ages. According to Carl Jung artists transcend the historical times in which they live. They speak directly to human hearts out of ancient perennial images. Their voices have a contemporary sound that resonates in harmony with all time. The dance medium can be traditional Classical Ballet, primitive ritualistic dancing, or any form of communication through movement. Great art speaks through myth, symbol, fantasy, religion, legend, and modern contemporary dissonance. It speaks from one heart to another, to the intra-personal and inter-personal of connectedness and relationship.

Whether or not we see it with Jung, as the impact of the summoning up of archetypal images, we are touched and often profoundly moved mysteriously by that which "speaks with a thousand voices."[3]

17

A Voice in the Wilderness

The impact of art as a vicarious experience is one of universal significance. We called works of art a means of communication. They touch the hearts of individuals by speaking profound existential truth. It seems to follow that the artist would also have a voice in society. It could be significantly more meaningful than might appear at first glance. We say that artists make a statement through the medium of their art form. Perhaps that is more obvious in drama, or literature, than dance. Yet, movement speaks loudly where words fail. Dance makes use of the symbols and images from both drama and literature.

Agnes de Mille speaks of a figure found throughout drama.

> They are the men who dare what for others would be impious or disrespectful. These are the middlemen, the liaison figures between human law and divine power. These people commune with the underground, speak to the dead, mock the King, and in doing so, hearten the common man. No society has ever tried to live without them. They have different names in

different cultures. They are always the same person, the voice of truth, the critic, the only possible approach to the Gods.[1]

In the Old Testament we find the figure of a prophet who was a spokesman for God, for the nation of Israel. In the biblical sense, prophets were persons who had a personal spiritual mission. They were signs in the world of the living presence of God and the creative action of the spirit. Prophets see with the "eyes of God", and speak out of that inspired vision. Most often their words were harsh reminders of the iniquities and failures of the people to be faithful to their God. Their message was a call to faith. They felt compelled to speak out, even against their own personal will. They were witnesses to social justice, God's love, and to holiness as a way of life. They spoke words that the people didn't want to hear and were often persecuted as a result. They were a powerfully influential voice in their society, and remain so in the lived experience of our Judeo-Christian heritage.

We are struck by the parallels between the prophet and the artist as seen in Carl Jung's insights. Earlier we mentioned that Jung felt that artists, whether aware of it or not, value their work beyond personal fate. He felt the artist's work reflects the spiritual needs of the society in which he lives. Artists are listening to an inner voice of love or anger, pain or joy. Their search for meaningful symbols and images are often inspired beyond their own intentions. The social significance of art can be found in the conflict of the individual artists. They make an effort to bring their own inner rhythms into harmony with the inconsistencies and imbalances of the external world in which they live. Jung sees the artist as "educating the spirit of the age, conjuring up forms in which the age is more lacking."[2] The messages are significant for generations. Great works of art always transcend their historical time and continue to sound the message of all time.

> The archetypal image of the wise man, the savior or redeemer, lies buried and dormant in man's unconscious since the dawn of culture; it is awakened whenever the times are out of joint

> and a human society is committed to serious error . . . These
> primordial images are numerous, but do not appear in the
> dreams of individuals or in works of art until they are called
> into being by the waywardness of the general outlook. When
> conscious life is characterized by one-sidedness and by a false
> attitude, then they are activated . . . one might say
> "instinctively" . . . and come to light in the dreams of individuals
> and the visions of artists and seers, thus restoring the psychic
> equilibrium of the epoch.[3]

Like prophets, artists also speak out of a sense of personal mission. This is profoundly indicated by the innovations of dancers and choreographers that significantly affected the development of the art form throughout history. They responded to the external realities of a historical time by reflecting the times in their work. But they also initiated whole movements in the life of dance to change the times. They worked to change human hearts, to create a new mythology, and envisioned dance as a means to physical, mental, and spiritual wholeness. They kept the art of Classical Ballet true to its own mythology and tradition. Great innovation called the primordial ritual back into focus. It is ritual that is so distinctly the voice of dancing throughout the ages of human existence. The experience of dance belongs to everyone. It can be a healing experience or a disruptive one, but it is always effective. The biblical prophets often spoke out against their own will with an inspiration attributed to God. The artist-dancer is inspired by an inner voice that may defy society in order to be heard. The inspired work of both the artist and the prophet always points beyond itself: back toward Tradition and forward toward Mystery.

III

A Contemplative Theory of Dance

After architecture has built the temple, and after the solid shape of the god has been placed in it by the hand of sculpture, the next step is for the sensuously present god to be confronted, in his own house, by the community.

Hegel

Perhaps we shall some day be strong enough and clear enough to see the shining beauty of even the darkest truth.

Will Durant

18

Moved by the Spirit

Spiritual traditions well understand that self-knowledge is the road we are to journey in our search for God. As individuals dancers experience dance within the context of their own inner reality, just as we do all of life's experience. That search for an inner reality is sought by many through personal growth as artists. It is a search for meaning in individual lives and ultimately, in all of human life. Dance is a way of discovering and becoming who we are. It expresses our deepest beliefs and makes our emotional experience visible. Through movement we communicate the human condition in all of its ambiguity and paradox from despair and ecstatic joy to simply giving praise for life. For many the challenge is to transcend human physical limitation through technical skill. We thereby release the human body into an expression of unlimited freedom of movement. There are words to express that freedom. Mastering the technique, we rise "above our work". It becomes easier as we become stronger. Movement is purified (more precise, cleaner, simplified) in the complexity of advanced technique. It sounds paradoxical to say that the more complicated the work in advancing levels the easier it becomes. The process is slow and requires self-discipline, consistency, and energy. In a sense, we receive from dance all that we are willing to give to her. As we mentioned in the first part of this study, for artists the creative process begins once they master their tools. In dance our tools are the human body. Once we are "above our work", our unique yet universal sense of being can be freely explored in movement. Ted Shawn used dance to express his search for the hidden God. For Isadora Duncan dance was a way of life—a religion. Martha Graham used dance to create a new mythology. From the primitive to the contemporary, dancing has always expressed the deepest realities of human life-experience.

In each chapter of our study, we have uncovered deeper dimensions of dance as an art form. By exploring different perspectives of human creativity, we broaden our understanding. Psychological insights into artists and the dance produce evidence of the mystery inherent in the nature of art and creativity. Carl Jung suggests that the artist's receptivity to archetypal imagery emerging from the unconscious mind contributes to the creative process. Karen Horney recognizes an innate movement in every person toward self-realization. Carl Rogers calls it "self-actualization". It is a process of becoming more authentically who we are, as unique, creative individuals. Spiritual writers and mystics experienced their search for God as a quest for wholeness. They sought ultimate spiritual freedom through a process of growing in self-knowledge. Saint Teresa of Avila said that to know yourself is to know God. Thomas Merton spoke of the True Self as opposed to the false images, attitudes, and expectations that prevent us from awakening to spiritual wholeness. All of them indicate a deepening of self awareness and self acceptance. By embracing and integrating what Jung calls the shadow side of our personalities, we grow in true compassion and ability to empathize with others. This process of growing into the fullness of our own humanity is vitally important in developing creative artists. We become more and more able to tap our inner-most sources of energy. We can define these realities as the psychological and spiritual requirements contributing to the effectiveness of great works of art.

The creative artist acts out of a spiritual realm. This consists

88

of collective, unconscious, primordial images and a profound connectedness to a source of creative energy. This energy flows through our own inner reality and deeply touches the inner reality of others. Artists may or may not speak consciously in spiritual terms. But they sense a connectedness to all that is universally human and personally relevant. This sense of connectedness is the heart of all human desire for relationship, harmony, and unity. These concepts cause us to reflect on the artist's openness to all that gives spiritual meaning to life. The freedom gained by the dancer in developing technical skill opens the door to simplicity and purity of expression. The emerging spiritual freedom of the True Self is transparently revealed in symbolic movement. The violence and effort of the work is transformed into a gentle tapping of the rich source of energy that sustains all of life. In spiritual terms, that source of energy is an expression of the spirit moving us to search for God. We hunger for the experience of our True Selves. As unique expressions of God, we are bound to one another in shared humanity by the power of love.

For dancers the experience of dance is one of human growth and development. By facing inner truths, we discover spiritual realities. We absorb the lessons of life into a wholeness of being that can be subtly reflected in different qualities of movement. The personality, temperament, responsiveness, and receptivity of dancers as individuals are reflected and exposed by their gifts of movement. The process of becoming a dancer—and a mature person—reminds us of the integration of personality that Jung explores in his work. Jung observed that the individual personality contains two opposing polarities—the masculine and feminine. He calls the dominant male archetype, animus. The dominant female archetype he termed, anima. In each person, the conscious archetypal identification is balanced by its opposite. In other words, a woman conscious of herself as female is balanced by her inner or unconscious aspects of the animus. Conversely, a man conscious of himself as male, is balanced by the anima.

Jung explores these images and their elusive qualities extensively. It is interesting to see how understanding this is relative to the experience of dance. Psychologically, the ideal is to integrate

89

the anima/animus image into a conscious and friendly relationship as part of the total personality. The more we become aware of our unconscious personal psyche, the more we realize the dichotomy between the conscious and unconscious aspects of our personalities. Even deeper than that, is the realm of the collective unconscious where the anima/animus resides. If a relationship with the collective unconscious is not recognized and established, the opposing forces will surface in very negative ways. The process is ongoing, since collective unconscious material has to be met, recognized, and related to, every time it appears to be present and operating. Jung's understanding of the individuation process, therefore, involves the integration of the anima/animus into a wholeness of personality. He speaks of the anima/animus as a shadow dwelling deep within the inner personality. The experience of dance is a process involving many aspects of growth, an integration of many opposing polarities.

In Part Two, we suggested that the Classical Ballet has a living created myth of its own. We used the image of the ballerina and her male partner as an example. We also explored the mythology related to Balanchine's image of dance as "woman". The training of the human body into a finely-tuned instrument of the dance corresponds to Jung's description of the integration of personality in the individuation process. The integration involved in developing as a dancer can be defined in relation to Jung's description of the qualities of anima/animus. The qualities of the animus are discriminating, focused, determined, and defined. The contrasting qualities of anima tend toward connectedness, relationship, and over-all values. In physical terms, the animus suggests strong, athletic, and forcefully energetic as opposed to the flexible, delicate, fluid, and graceful anima. The balance of personality qualities as well as the integration of physical qualities is personified in both male and female dancers.

The physical instrument must be muscularly strong and athletic in order to present itself as flexible and delicate. It must have the power to explode with energy, while simultaneously appearing effortless and graceful. The strongest dancers represent the most feminine qualities in movement. The focus, definition, and determination of personality must be visually integrated into the fluidity, connectedness, and wholeness of the movements. In essence the training is the same for male and female dancers. It seems profoundly significant that dancers are called to such extreme integration, yet, quite understandably when seen in the light of their calling. Dancers re-present in movement the emotional texture and quality of an infinite spectrum of possibilities in music. They dramatize real-life experiences, ideal qualities of legendary heroes and heroines, and multiple images and symbols of choreographic fantasy. They meet the demand to embody the essence of what is purely and simply beautiful. Spiritually, the dancer cannot reflect a deity that does not embody all that is male and female, strong and weak, powerful and vulnerable. Dancers are the embodiment of every paradox inherent in the mystery of what it is to be a human being. All this in order to reach out and touch the hearts of others, that they too may be moved by the spirit of the dance.

19

Aesthetics: A Philosophy of Dance

Philosophers through the ages have explored the underlying principles of art, calling their philosophy, aesthetics. Aesthetics is a study or theory of art or beauty. It is interesting that the art of dance has not been specifically explored by philosophers. That is an invitation to attempt a philosophical exploration of our own in this study—to apply the principles of aesthetics to the dance. It may even provide the philosophic perspective of dance that was previously missing. Thus far we have set the stage historically, grounding our understanding of dance as an art form. We explored the meaning of Form versus forms, Tradition versus traditions, and classical versus romantic in the development of the Classical Ballet. Reaching into the realm of symbol, image, and myth in relation to dance and art, we discovered the universality of archetypal imagery as part of the creative process.

Philosophy, by definition, is concerned with underlying principles, concepts, and ideas. Plato was the first to suggest that a philosophical study considers the universality of things, rather than their concrete form. He said that the truth of art was not to be found in the work of art, but rather in the essence of goodness, truth, and beauty in themselves. The starting point for a philosophy of art, therefore, is in the idea of the beautiful. Aesthetics is not concerned with natural beauty, but with human creativity and artistic creation.

Hegel, one of the most important philosophers of the romantic movement in the nineteenth century, is considered the founder of modern systematic aesthetics. Hegel considers art as an expression of a spiritual content that is also the content and vocation of both religion and philosophy. He defines art in three significant modes: the symbolic, classical, and romantic. Hegel sees the arts as an expression of intuition and ideas that can reveal the philosophy and religion of nations. So far, these concepts follow our direction very appropriately. Next, he indicates a progression of five major art forms: architecture, as the most solid, and enclosing three dimensional space, is seen as symbolic in its nature; sculpture, which fills space rather than enclosing it, is directly expressed in classical perfection; the perspective of the three romantic arts, painting, music, and literature, is internal. The symbolic and classical are external. Music, which takes art out of a spatial dimension altogether, is seen as the most internal of artistic expressions. It reaches into a range of subjective feelings in great depth.

The three modes of art, symbolic, classical, and romantic are seen as the relationship between the content and form that actualizes the Idea of the beautiful. We can call those three basic relationships the process that transforms the Idea into its external artistic representation. In an effort to express the truth of symbolic art, Hegel turns to the images of the ancient Egyptians. He considers them as the first authentically artistic people, because they recognized a dichotomy between nature and spirit. As an example of symbolic art, he cites the pyramids. Their external shape hides the labyrinthian underground passages that give them their true internal or spiritual meaning. In essence, Hegel views the symbolic as an effort to express an inner spiritual meaning by giving it external shape. Because the effort has the intent to express what is infinite, and therefore inexpressible, the attempt is always imperfect. He turns to the Greek culture to find the epitome of the classical art form. The perfect unity of content and shape expresses true beauty. It was seen by the Greeks as visible in the human form, which is the true shape, or temple, of the spirit. "Where spirit is art's content, the human body, as spirit's dwelling place, must be its form, declares Hegel.[1] Thus, the Greek gods and goddesses, heroes and heroines, were represented in human forms. Greek sculpture is the personification of the human spirit in idealized artistic form. Here, Hegel sees a limit in the classical ideal which must "express itself fully in the natural form of man, without suggesting some higher significance that might transcend sensory expression."[2] Therefore, he calls romantic art "the self-transcendence of art itself."

Hegel considers that art forms have a common basis in their striving for universal truth. Romantic art is whatever is universally human, expressed from the perspective of a deep subjective spirituality. The relationships described above are found in each of five major art forms; architecture, sculpture, painting, music, and literature. I suggest that we consider dance as a sixth major art form and attempt to qualify our philosophy appropriately. We have seen Hegel's three modes of expression as the relationship of content to form. If we look closely at the description of Hegel's five major art forms, we can recognize something explicit within the dance in each of them. Once again, relationship is the key to our understanding. Considering each of the five major forms separately will help to clarify these relationships.

The spatial dimension of architecture is defined as the ideal form of the symbolic mode. It can be clearly seen in the structure and external shape that gives dance a concrete or solid appearance. In its external shape or form, choreography can be described as enclosing three dimensional space in the same way that Hegel describes architecture. The relationship of the content of the ballet to the external form or shape of the choreography can be seen as an example of the symbolic mode or process. In Part Two, we described the symbolic as a representation of something else. Visually its content can even be entirely absent. The shape or external form of a choreographic piece stands visually in the place of its hidden symbolic meaning. The choreographer may or may

95

not intend to concretely reveal these subtleties of meaning. Perhaps the architecture of the ballet, like a pyramid, will enclose the three dimensional space visually and leave its labyrinthian depths of meaning to the imagination of the audience. We might suggest that the architecture of a ballet is comparable to what we call the craft. It designates the visual patterns and intertwining of the dancers as they move through space. Thus, they enclose it three dimensionally.

As dancers we inherit the perspective of Greek culture in its adoration of the human form. Hegel says that if the content of art is spiritual, its most perfect or truest form is the human body in which the spirit dwells. The relationship of content to form is the classical mode. It is the perfect unity of content and shape, and expresses true beauty. Hegel calls sculpture the essence of classical perfection because it fills space rather than enclosing it. The human body of individual dancers is shaped and physically molded by the classical training into a sculptured and ideal form. The body, as the human instrument of the dance, resembles the ideal of Greek sculpture. It captured a perfection of line and symmetry into a perfect balance of form, to personify the human spirit in the gods and goddesses, heroes and heroines of classic Greek culture and mythology. As we shall see, the Classical Ballet itself, as a traditional art form, remains quite true to Hegel's definition of the classical mode. Hegel sees in the very qualities that define the classical mode its own limitation. He turns to the romantic mode of art to more fully express the spiritual depth he seeks to reveal as present in art.

Hegel's romantic arts brings us into familiar territory. The striving for universal truth and self-transcendence via the romantic mode is the attempt to give artistic representation to an infinite range of subjective human experiences. Hegel points to the Christian paintings of the sixteenth and seventeenth centuries as exemplifying the romantic mode of art. They are also the transitional art form between the three dimensional spatial arts and those forms that take art out of the spatial dimension altogether. For Hegel the epitome of romantic art is a representation of the universal quality of Christian love. It expresses the human soul in its passionate striving for unity. As an Ideal, it expresses life as it is experienced in the depth of the human heart. Romantic art need not remain solely in the realm of religious representation. It can represent nature or scenes of secular life as long as they visibly express deep internal response of the human soul. Thus, romantic art is a visual representation of the artist's response to life and experience as it reaches out to evoke a universal response in others. So far, we recognize a mutuality in the essential quality of both painting and dance. We can reiterate our earlier view that dance easily falls into the category of the romantic mode of art. The point where dance and painting are most dramatically connected is in the realm of color. Just as the painter creates appearances by playing upon the visual shading of light and dark, so the choreographer creates visual effects and appearances with colors in costuming, decors, and stage lighting. The mood or emotional and spiritual climate is set for the ballet just as it is in painting. This understanding was recognized with innovative insight by the Russian impressario, Serge Diaghilev. He envisioned ballet as an integration of painting, music and dance. The artist's mastery in painting is the revelation of spiritual depth and intense meaning within a two dimensional milieu. Artists can create the appearance of movement and even a three dimensional perspective by the masterful use of color. Dance can as easily be described as a "painting in movement", as "visual music".

We move into the realm of music and poetry via painting. Painting is the transitional mode of romantic art. It moves us gently from the spatial dimension of external artistic expression to an internal artistic perspective with no visible spatial dimension. "Good ballets move in measured space and time," says George Balanchine. The relationship of internal and external rhythms in time and space gives a mathematical dimension to these non-spatial arts. Balanchine made the mathematical relationships in poetry and music visible in the dance. He found this to be the ultimate relationship of ballet to music. Remember that the three modes of art are the process that transforms the idea into its artistic representation. At the heart of poetry and music is rhythm. Rhythm immediately calls to mind an entirely new artistic dimension: it reminds us of the basic pulse and energy that sustains life. It holds life in constant motion and underlies a harmonic balance of relationships. Hegel sees poetry as the most universal artistic medium because it can effectively use symbolic, classical, or romantic expression as the relationship of its content to form. The medium of poetry is the imagination, which contains the possibility of unlimited content. In the romantic mode art succeeds in transcending itself. He speaks of poetry as a form of knowing and experiencing as I speak of dance. The common element in poetry, dance, and music is rhythm.

Dance holds its own as a major art form. The Classical Ballet would be seen by Hegel as primarily identified with the classical mode of expression. It seeks and finds the perfect unity of content and form. The limitation lies within the classical form itself because it does not suggest a higher significance, according to Hegel. In Part Two, we described Jung's mode of creativity that produces a work of art complete in itself. The Classical Ballet as a system of vocabulary used to express a pure visual representation of the musical score becomes an exemplar of the classical mode. It also exemplifies this mode of creativity, as Jung describes it. This ballet is complete in itself. It remains entirely true to the form, content, and structure of the music. Its sole intention is to make the structure of the music visible. This is as representative of the classical mode of art as Hegel's Greek sculpture. However, we have also seen how dance and the Classical Ballet can include the symbolic, classical, and romantic in its artistic expression. Even Balanchine discerned a higher significance within the range of the Classical Ballet as an artistic medium. In his description of classic and romantic ballet, cited in Part One of this study, he explains how the theme of a classic ballet can be romantic, mythological or realistic. All three of Hegel's modes of artistic expression can be seen in the Classical Ballet as the process of relating the content of a ballet to its form. All five of his major art forms are incorporated into dance in structure, form, color, content and quality of expression. By describing his major art forms, Hegel describes the dance.

The relationship of content to form as an expression of goodness, truth, and beauty will lead us still more deeply into our aesthetics of dance.

20

Goodness, Truth and Beauty

It is interesting that the progression of art forms, in the philosophy of art that we have been following, was written by Hegel more than one hundred and fifty years ago. America was hardly established as a nation. We inherited European philosophy along with its religion and art. In Hegelian thought, the human concepts of goodness, truth, and beauty are sought deeply and profoundly. He states that religion seeks the highest Good. Philosophy explores the highest Truth. Art strives to attain to pure Beauty. As Plato suggests, it is the essence of these qualities that we hope to perceive, and in some way, accept, understand, and experience. In other words, the theologian, mystic, or spiritual person seeks to know goodness experientially in, of, and through itself. The philosopher reaches through cognition and the conceptualization of ideas toward the Ideal or Truth of all that exists. The artist works to evoke imagery giving shape, form, and visual or auditory expression to the ideal of the Beautiful.

Are these understandings of religion, philosophy and art still meaningful in our contemporary society? Are they universal and immutable values? Or do they change with human growth and development? Has our human capacity for boundless creativity altered how we as late twentieth century explorers experience life and perceive its ultimate value and meaning? Perhaps Hegelian philosophy serves us best as a starting point from which to begin our research into the development of human art forms from a philosophical perspective. It can expand, grow, and broaden our awareness of our contemporary experience of life.

Does the essence of what is most human change with our new and expanded world view? Are the ideals of goodness, truth, and beauty alterable realities? Or do human beings and creative artists continue to strive for the Ideal that at root remains forever and eternal? Are we conditioned by our religion, philosophy, and art? Or, do we shape and remold them in the continual process of change in evolving human life? We have approached some of these questions earlier in this study. It appears that we shape and are shaped in varying degrees by external and environmental phenomena. We are also affected by biological, emotional, physical, and spiritual experience and inheritance. Communication has been a pervasive theme in this work. I, therefore, suggest that modern psychology is the addition that twentieth century Western civilization offers to augment our theme. Along with religion, philosophy, and art, psychology is a creative expression of our universal human need to understand and communicate who we are in relation to our multi-cosmic world. The additional perspective of psychology has been introduced in various ways throughout this study. Its appropriateness can be clearly seen if we consider that by defini-tion it is a developing modern science of mind and behavior. We have already explored psychological theories of human creativity. I choose to consider psychotherapy as an art. It attempts, in its process through experiencing and understanding, to explore and enhance our capacity as human beings for authentic relationship and communication. Seen in this light, psychology presents itself as a late twentieth century healing art. It offers yet another perspec-tive from which to view goodness, truth, and beauty.

The twentieth century modern American dancer, Ted Shawn,

gave us a Creed that I quoted at the beginning of this study. He believed that dance has the power to heal, mentally and physically. True education in the art of dance is education of the whole person. The relationship of content to form in art is the process of integration and reconciliation that creates universal communication. The conscious striving of the art of dance and the art of psychotherapy are parallel experiences. They are both healing relationships toward oneself and others, mentally and physically, through the process of developing communication. The process of knowing and experiencing our physical bodies through movement and dance is healing, integrating, and reconciling. In the process of learning to feel the most intricate and subtle movements of each part of the human body, we come to know and experience ourselves with increased awareness. We come into relationship with our human form in a deeper and more vital way. We are in touch with a most sensory human experience of being.

Modern psychologists have discovered sensory experience as essential to a sense of well-being. Newborn babies—if deprived of physical contact through touching, holding, and caressing—can die. We are totally dependent on another to touch us physically in order to begin to relate to our own physical selves. It is in those earliest moments of life that healing and wholeness for us, as persons, begins. Physical sensation is essential to health. When it is explored and experienced in dance, it becomes a healthy knowing of oneself. When it develops into a means of self-expression, it begins to touch on relationship in terms of communication. The relationship of content to form, in art, is a process of arriving at universal communication. It is similar to an ideal intra-personal or subjective relationship in which we can fully experience our feelings, become aware of them, and authentically communicate or express them to another. We begin to touch on the truth of art, dance, and psychology. Here, the reconciliation of content to form is what we know and experience and finally communicate. It is the greatest truth, given the artistic medium through which we choose to express that truth. In that sense, philosophy, which seeks the highest Truth, finds in art its reconciliation and expression.

In dance, the human form gives its own deepest truth a physical reality. In the Classical Ballet, the perfect unity of content to form finds a traditional truth that we would clearly see as a fine example of Hegel's classical mode of artistic expression. The intuition we have for that expression of truth, or authenticity, is an intrinsic aspect of this study. It is evident that the mental and physical healing that dance offers us is found in part by the authenticity of our intra-personal relationship with ourselves both mentally and physically. The remainder of the healing effect is in the authentic expression and communication of this relationship through dance as our artistic medium. Giving visual, physical expression through movement to my emotional and spiritual reality is the beginning of the healing and reconciliation. The greatness of dance as an art form lies in its ability to give expression to the truth of its content and form. It expresses the truth of the whole human person through the ritual of symbolic, classical, and romantic movement.

As the temple of the spirit, the human body of the dancer serves as a liaison between spirit and nature. This role is similar to the prophet or priest serving as a liaison between God and His people. The dancer's body is the voice. It is the visual re-presentation or artistic expression of internal spiritual truths. Religion seeks the highest Good which dance reveals as hidden deep within the temple of the human form. Dance expresses the movement of human souls. At the turn of the twentieth century, we found great innovators of the dance re-vitalizing it. They instilled her with soul, spirit, and individuality in response to an impersonal, technologically developing society. As Jung suggests, psychologically this movement in dance was serving as a healing artistic force. It was calling our essential humanity into integration with our developing modern society. The healing process, that seeks authentic integration of feelings into awareness and expression, also includes pastoral care of spiritual values. Close observance of body language indicates unconscious feelings. Therapies have developed called movement therapy. They seek to bring the physical constrictedness and physically observable tensions in natural movements into full awareness. These indications of personality disorders are treated by freeing the movements and thereby entering into the healing process.

As most of us are well aware, facial expressions, postures, and physical gestures often concretely reveal our unvoiced hidden agendas. To search for the highest Good in, of, and through goodness itself is a religious quest that is shared by all artistic traditions. In the process of creativity, a psychological phenomenon produces increased awareness, integration, and a fullness of human expression. It is tapping into a source of goodness that is healing and wholesome. True education in dance puts us intimately in touch with our physical being. Through the process or relationship of its content to form, education in dance more fully integrates our psychology with our physical reality. It expresses the convictions of our hearts. In this way, true education in dance is a healing of the whole person. Increasing awareness and coming more fully alive and present to the fullness of our own physical, psychological, and spiritual humanity is a process that, in itself, speaks of health and well-being. It presents as a sense of goodness, pointing toward its own source, the highest Good.

Hegel describes the ultimate objective of art as a perfecting of human activity or creativity. It is a perfecting of the art of human making, doing, or creating. The striving for pure beauty or the essence of the Ideal of beauty can be the creating of beautiful objects, movements, sounds, or literary images. However we may speak of what is beautiful, or perceive beauty as a quality, we experience it in, of, and through the ideal of Beauty itself. We may not always agree on our ideas or perceptions or the beautiful. If the striving of art, however, is for the purest beauty, then there must be a universal Ideal of beauty. It is the archetype that great art expresses in such a way that all persons are profoundly touched by it or can in some way find identity within it. I choose to explore beauty, therefore, as the process of creative activity. Beauty is the unfolding or revealing and reconciling aspect of the relationship of artistic content to artistic form. In the classical mode of art, the perfect expression of artistic content to form produces a visual representation of the ideal of pure beauty. Balanchine said that the Classical Ballet is beautiful in itself. He implied that, in experiencing it, we will be affected by the beautiful. In seeking pure beauty, we come into relationship with her. We recognize the content of great art

103

within the confines of its form. That recognition is a knowledge that can only be perceived experientially within the process of relationship. We describe our human relationships as beautiful. Beauty is reflected in the eyes of those we know well and love. We see beauty in tender gestures. We are often affected by natural beauty and feel a profound connection to nature. We all know the experience of "beautiful", although we may not give it formal expression. In fact, we cannot describe or talk about goodness, truth, or beauty. We can only perceive them in our experiencing. We know, by experience, what feels good, true, and beautiful. They are profound sensory human experiences. They also speak of the human creative process in our relationship in, of, and through them.

In dance, beauty finds expression in multiple ways that are unique to dance itself. Experiencing beauty through expressive movement reminds us of the primordial beginnings of human consciousness that we described in the first chapters of this study. To primitive people, the psyche appeared as the sign of life. It was both the source and prime mover of life. It included movement, and moving force. What is more, this experience of the psyche was conceived of as having a life of its own. In Greek mythology, Psyche was the princess who was loved by Cupid and, according to the myth, her beauty aroused the hatred and jealousy of Aphrodite. With the aid of Cupid's love, however, she overcame the venomous hatred of Aphrodite, and was immortalized and united to Cupid forever. Symbolically, Psyche is a representation of the human soul purified by the pain of passion and trial, and thus prepared for eternal happiness. Hegel found that Christian art in the Middle Ages expressed the epitome of romantic art because it re-presented the ideal of Christian love. Traditional art is a means of reflecting the human psyche. Through the use of symbolism, which is a mechanism of tapping into primordial, archetypal imagery, it reveals the earliest human experience of life. Seen in the light of contemporary psychology the primitive experience of the psyche seems to be simplistic and naive. A closer look reveals that the depth of our new knowledge explores that primitive sense. We discover a world of autonomous collective unconscious symbols, and a psychic activity that indeed has a life of its own. It is into this psychic life, through relationship in, of, and through expressive creative activity, that dance gives form to the beautiful. Beautiful form is a reflective expression of a stream of psychic life. It is at once our source, and our means of becoming who we are as human beings. The beautiful is a reminder of who we are in the very depth of our being. Those who dance, and view dance, come into a unique relationship with beauty because the human body is our instrument. It is both an internal expression and an external, visible communication. It is both a personal relationship, and a communal relationship.

Dance, as an expression of life, is primitive because it involves the totality of body, mind, and spirit. All the qualities of personality, psychology, and emotional feelings are made visible through the movements of the human body. When a ballet is beautiful, all those who participate experience that beauty and become an integral part of it. Beauty is made visible. Thus the relationship of content to form in dance is a unique experience in the traditional arts. Beauty is expressed uniquely in dance by the ability of the human form to give visual expression to those qualities in music, painting, and literature. We see the inter-relationship of all art forms and contents as integrally connected to dance. In its most complete form, dance has a unique ability to present beauty from a multitude of human perspectives. The epitome of art is to express the essence of goodness, truth and beauty, in and of, themselves. Our Greek princess, the goddess Psyche, is the personification of the human soul, immortalized by Cupid's love. She is a magnificent symbol and clue to the universal expression of human love. Psyche, the human soul immortalized by love, represents the total human personality. She points toward love in all creative processes. The process of relating content to form, through goodness, truth, and beauty, is uniquely expressed in dance.

21

Harmony, Synchronization and Unity

The task of the first stage of life is to discover our relationship to the environment. This external process is underscored by recent scientific/medical studies on the left and right hemispheres of the brain. These contemporary studies seek to reconcile questions concerning the relationship of the physiological/biological brain to what has been called, the human "soul". The left hemisphere of the brain governs our ability to discriminate and develop consciousness. Our first developmental tasks focus on these functions of the left/brain. The right hemisphere of the brain is responsible for the creative imagination. It is active in the development of our intuition, fantasy, play, symbolic images, and myth. The transition from the first half of life to the second is often experienced as a painful search for inner meaning and internal reconciliation. The well-developed conscious and rational left/brain is challenged by our unconscious into further integration. The right/brain allows our spiritual, religious, and artistic personalities to emerge. Difficult transitions during the human life cycle develop our capacity to grow creatively. Contemporary scientific/medical studies invite us to seek to develop both sides of the human brain as fully as possible. Nurturing human creativity, however, goes beyond the realm of science and enters into the process of art.

Throughout this study we have touched on the qualities of harmony, synchronization, and unity in various ways. Essentially, we have been exploring our relationship to a world of sound and rhythm to which we are attuned before we are even born. Becoming creatively, and therefore rhythmically, in-tune with the flow of energy that sets life into motion, is an integrating process of human growth and development. It is necessary for healthy inter-relationships with ourselves, others, and our environment. Spontaneous primitive dance as religious ritual was an expression of human symbiotic union and an identification of spirit with nature. It expressed the search for universal harmony through a synthesis of movement, rhythm, and sound. These basic human needs arise out of existing universal energies.

In music, harmony provides the textural element in the combination of tones. It provides the over-all impression of texture. Harmony provides the "feel", "touch", or "fabric" of the music by the way it integrates sounds. The elements that create the sound of music interconnect with the energies created by the rhythmical movements of the dancers. This produces a visual effect of unity within the over-all thematic content of the dance. The impact creates a magic synthesis of newness in great works of art. Silvano Arieti describes this as the creative person's ability to conceive a totality, or unity. This ability remains the secret of the individual creative personality. It participates in the mystery of creativity itself. We are reminded that creativity is dependent on the human imagination. Synchronizing simultaneous visual and auditory images is crucial to dance as an art form. Human beings possess unique abilities to play with and explore these visual and auditory images. The scope of this ability is astounding.

Comparative mythology opens a door in our journey. It ushers us into the creative process of dance. The art of choreography munificently draws upon vast dimensions of collective, universal, and profoundly meaningful symbols. What is the significance of this

108

gathering of symbolic image and myth into the realm of dance? We seek to coincide dissonance. The artist strives for unity in a world torn asunder by discord, disharmony and apparently irreconcilable opposites. Human consciousness develops from the primitive, collective, and unitive, to the contemporary, individual, and uniquely other. This increasing movement toward expansion, complexity, growth, and awareness is in direct opposition to a simultaneous universal process called entropy. In this process, matter and energy in the universe are ultimately decomposing into a state of inertness. Our human experience of life, and the larger universe, is entropic. Living seems to move us through stages from birth, to maturity, to ultimately slowing, decaying, and dying. I am proposing that within the process of creativity a principle is recognized indicating a movement in life, away, rather than toward, entropy. By tapping into energy that evolves, expands, and ultimately transcends, we are in-tune with a life rhythm, or current of life-giving force. That force moves each of us to desire, and seek, synchronization, harmony, and unity. We strive to transcend symbiotic re-union and nirvanic yearnings.

Our deeper longing is for a conjunction of opposing forces at-one, in, of, and through, the other. Nothing is lost or diminished in this expression of unity. We long to become, yet already are, an expression of our own unique, transcendent selves. Dancers are drawn into an artistic creative process that paradoxically enhances uniqueness and likeness simultaneously. It is an evolving, rather than diminishing, experience. Dance reveals some distinct examples of creative process at work in this way. What is strong appears fragile. Dancers appear as one, by collectively moving in unison. Bodies defy gravity by appearing to stop moving in the air. Music appears to be visible. Dancers land out of flying leaps so softly that they make no sound. Our bodies move so smoothly they appear to glide, or be made of rubber material. Human beings appear to be solid geometric shapes and forms. Abstract qualities of movement include hidden symbolic meanings. Deeply felt emotions are visible in physical movements. These examples are a product of the craft and skills inherent in the art form. They are intentional creations of illusion. We are about to explore our earlier hints of universal tensions and polarities expressed in creative artistic endeavors. The first aspect of our aesthetic theory concerns dualities. The second concerns more contemplative reflections on dance in terms of creative unitive experience and transcendence. We will be involved with the former for the remainder of this chapter.

Our aesthetic exploration in terms of dualities and polarities is congruent with our Hegelian philosophical model. This philosophy continues to influence our contemporary thought and expressive ideas. The prevailing attitude, or "mind", of any era affects all facets of life experience. That includes its artistic expressions. They respond to that "climate", or environment, by reflecting, opposing, or changing it. Hegel saw art as a creative means of transcending the paradoxes of the dualities that dominated the thinking of his time. In all human experience, Hegel saw the inevitability of its opposite. Therefore, art was a means of relating to opposites by uniting them, and thereby creating a higher, and more complex whole. For Hegel, the evolutionary process was a continuing development of contrasting realities that finally merge in reconciliation. They thereby transcend their original duality. He saw the romantic mode of artistic expression as a means of art transcending itself by reconciling dualities in the truth of artistic expression. The problem of dualities, and the need, therefore, for reconciliation, dominated the interpretations of human experience at the time. Hegel saw the arts in a context of dichotomy between matter and spirit.

This concept of the universe only belongs to our Western life experience and thought. Comparative mythology reveals the source of this dilemma. In Oriental philosophy, everything, though apparently changing, remains fixed in an eternal state of harmony. The entire cosmos is a state of Being, rather than a process of Becoming. With this mentality, the secret, or mystery, is known. There is no conflict between Creator and creature. Our struggle in Western civilization is between the spiritual and the sensual.

This conflict continues to emerge in contemporary psychology and in our search for human identity. Our mythology, religious ritual, and arts continue to reflect our human need to establish a relationship between Creator and creature. This struggle with polarities is seen in ancient Greek mythology. Masculine power is symbolized by Dionysius standing opposite to the classical feminine beauty of Apollo. Jung's archetypal symbols are anima and animus. He saw the tension between polarities as a source of psychic energy producing creative expression and artistic activity. In our culture we continue to struggle with the inherited mythology and religious conflicts of the past. Simultaneously, through contemporary explorations of the arts and sciences, psychologists are coming to new understandings of polarities. They are seen in terms of human growth, and the energy that is created in an effort to balance polar tensions. Today we are more inclined to visualize the conscious and unconscious, the spiritual and sensual, the internal and external, and the rational and intuitive, as two sides of the same coin. They are dualities contained within the same essential principle. The common component in comparative religions is the effort to bring opposites together. In the religious sense, it is creating a balance between the sacred and profane, the eternal and temporal, or God and humanity. An extraordinary amount of human creativity has been evoked by this conflict of duality and opposition.

We are searching for insight into the human experience, seen in artistic expressions, that seeks to synthesize in order to create a sense of harmony and unity. We inherit from the late Middle Ages an attempt to find synchronization, harmony, and unity through philosophical and theological thought, as well as religious mystical experience. The influence of our medieval Western European ancestors, and how they perceived their struggle with opposing forces, remains alive in our contemporary religious communities and modern humanistic philosophy. It inevitably finds its way into our artistic expressions. The art of dance, as our ground of experience in this study, resonates with ancient as well as contemporary issues of dualities and polarities.

The question of duality was documented concretely by the religious experiences of individuals in the Middle Ages. From the theological and spiritual perspective, the conflict is clearly evident.

111

We inherit two apparently opposing European ideologies of God as Immanent, and God as Transcendent. Our model is the thirteenth century Saint Francis of Assisi, and the metaphysical reflections of his follower, Saint Bonaventure. This model allows us to enter into the mystery of human creativity more concretely. Bonaventure's system of thought is a model of synthesis. Its process exists within our richly inherited tradition of Western thought.

Our Judeo-Christian heritage places the artist within the mystical framework of God's Immanence in creation. This corresponds appropriately to the vision of Saint Francis. His spirituality remains an outstanding exemplar of this mystical tradition. He envisioned the reflection of God manifest in every creature, and in all of creation. Judeo-Christian philosophy also incorporates the "otherness", or transcendence of God. This is clearly evident in the Christian, Jewish and Islamic religious traditions. Our traditional art forms thus appear to align with a specific mystical spirituality. The soul's journey toward ultimate union in God is sought through the senses. This approach to spirituality can be seen as a coincidence of opposites. It is a theme to which we are already exposed through Hegelian philosophy and Jungian psychology. Bonaventure's system of thought reflects the Franciscan spiritual tradition. Ewert Cousins describes it as a model of synthesis. He calls it a tradition of "mutually affirming complementarity."[1] This system of thought resembles the contemporary principles of Taoism in Yin-Yang, and the thought of twentieth century Jesuit priest and paleontologist, Teilhard de Chardin. Teilhard saw a law throughout the universe through which true uniqueness is achieved by creative union. It is also seen in the classical Christian doctrine of the Trinity, envisioned by Bonaventure as a model of the coincidence of opposites. Cousins describes a mode of understanding this concept by extending it to a "coincidence of mutually affirming complementarity". The more intimately the opposites are united, the more distinctly they are differentiated, and seen to complement one another.

Christianity itself fits into this mode of understanding unity and difference, due to the doctrine of the Incarnation. The Incarnation forms the basis of Bonaventure's entire theological vision. Briefly, the doctrine of the Incarnation is the mystery which views the ultimate exemplar of God's immanence in creation as visible in the person of Jesus. Hegelian philosophy reflects the medieval doctrine of the Trinity. It is the construct for his entire philosophy. We can place the dance within this spiritual model and interpretation of duality. The Classical Ballet as a traditional system relates to the tradition of a coincidence of mutually affirming complementarity evident in Bonaventure's system of thought.

The influence of Western European philosophical and theological thinking upon the development of Classical Ballet cannot be ignored. The system of thought expressed by Bonaventure, as specifically Christian, also suggests universal implications. It forms a basis for a broader world view of common religious experience. This system is as relevant to human experience, and the nature of human creativity today, as it was in the Middle Ages, and will continue to be in the future.

As early as 500 B.C., Greek philosophy reflected two opposing views of existence. Parmenides' unchangeable Being contrasted with Heraclitus' theory of ceaseless Becoming. These two opposing views continue to be a source of dialogue and interpretation in contemporary philosophical thinking and Christian theology. Responding to this dilemma, Bonaventure's principle finds in God's Transcendence the root of God's Immanence.

> By seeing transcendence itself as fecundity, and by situating fecundity within the Trinity, Bonaventure has safeguarded God's transcendence and at the same time has provided a solid basis for God's immanence in the world."[2]

All of creation has an eternal existence within the interior life of the Trinity. Bonaventure calls the second person of the Trinity (the Son), the Word, which expresses all that the Father can make, and therefore all that can be made.

> These 'eternal reasons' within the Son are the ontological ground of each individual creature. Thus Bonaventure can say

that things have a three-fold existence: They exist in the Eternal Art (in the Son), they exist also in matter, and they exist within the mind. The most important dimension of their existence is in the Eternal Art, within the Son as Image and Word of the Father... Through their exemplaristic grounding in the Word, all creatures reflect God and lead man to God... in reflecting God, their own individuality is intensified. While being intimately related to God, they remain radically themselves. Bonaventure holds that within the Word there are archetypes of each individual thing, not merely universal ideas. This is Bonaventure's way of affirming the Franciscan sense of the importance of individuality and the value of uniqueness... In the coincidence of opposites between God and creatures, the opposites are maintained and intensified by their coincidence. For Bonaventure, all the types of the coincidence of opposites—whether in the Trinity or in the world—are opposites of mutually affirming complementarity. That means that there is real opposition: both poles remain intact and are not absorbed in the other. God is not absorbed in the world, nor the world in God. But it means also that these opposites actually coincide, that they are internally related and not merely juxtaposed externally. The opposites interpenetrate and by this interpenetration intensify their uniqueness... In Bonaventure, God is eminently creative independently of the world: but because of the eminent reality of the eternal reasons, he is most intimately involved in the world... Bonaventure affirms God's immanence without threatening his transcendence... Bonaventure's doctrine of exemplarism is situated in his Trinitarian theology. If the world participates in the mystery of the dynamic Trinity, then it shares in the unbounded creativity and the eternal novelty of the generation of the Son."[3]

In *Bonaventure and the Coincidence of Opposites*, Cousins explores Bonaventure's system in relation to twentieth century thought and ecumenism. I bring Bonaventure's system into dialogue with a contemporary classical art form. Franciscan spirituality is the container for dance, movement, and the human body as an instrument of creative expression. Dance is the most logical archetype for a dialogue between God's immanence and transcendence. Can we see the Dance within God as dynamic and eternal Art? In the high Middle Ages Saint Francis of Assisi's spirituality was grounded in his devotion to the humanity of Christ. This high point of exemplarism allows us to address the issue of dance as an expression of the sacred. We place our contemporary creative expression of the Classical Ballet system within a sacred tradition. This is the sacred tradition in the Western European milieu, out of which the Classical Ballet system developed. It inherits a mode of thinking that has affected its mode of expression. The sacredness, inherent in all human creativity, is expressed through the Classical Ballet tradition as it has developed into a major contemporary art form. Cousins' "coincidence of mutually affirming complementarity", is the cornerstone of Bonaventure's philosophy, metaphysics, and theology. The Classical Ballet system exemplifies a creative expression of this long tradition of Western thought. Robley Whitson points out that Bonaventure's theological vision of the Trinity, "revealed through the book of creation, the book of Scripture, and the book of life", can be interpreted to mean that all human experience is a reflection of God.[4]

In part one of this study, we described the Classical Ballet as a system of vocabulary, or a "dictionary". It is also a method of instruction and the grammar for combinations of steps and phrases of movement. In this sense, the Classical Ballet system is the essential form revealing the shape and nature of movements. The evolution of human creativity brings dance from a primitive and ritualistic expression of life to a refined and progressively more stylized and formal expression. This highly technical art form continues to struggle to maintain a balance between the extremes of its essentially spiritual nature and its extraordinary technical development. In light of this conflict, I identify the Classical Ballet system as an archetypal Ideal. The Ideal image transcends its own technique. It also transcends its dependence on the individual and the collective experience of its human artists. The Dance encompasses them while uniquely identifying them in their artistic creations. It sustains its eminently real spiritual identity and appears to have existence in its own right.

In dialogue with Bonaventure's system of thought, the Classical Ballet system is seen as Transcendence, or Being, in much the same way as Bonaventure envisions Christianity. This is an overall mode of understanding unity and difference in the light of the coincidence of mutually affirming complementarity. Bonaventure sees the most important dimension of the three-fold existence of things as their existence within the Eternal Art. This is the "unbounded creativity and the eternal novelty of the generation of the Son".

God's absolute Transcendence and self-sufficiency, personified by the Ideal of the Classical Ballet archetype, reconciles God's self-communicating Immanence in creation through a coincidence of mutually affirming complementarity. The Classical Ballet Ideal contains within it the vocabulary, the method of instruction, and the grammar. These provide a continuous source of creative possibilities for the spiritual expression of itself. There is a tension between polarities that coincides in the relationship between the spiritual content of a Ballet and its classical form, or system, of dance expression. This tension is created in the process of technically perfecting movements, and intimately uniting them to the spiritual content of the Ballet, without the loss of either the technique or the spirit. "The more intimately these opposites are united, the more distinctly they are differentiated, and are seen to compliment one another." God's immanence is implicit within the process of relating the spiritual content of a ballet to its artistic form. Our human relationship to spiritual content is an internal process. Our relationship to the artistic form is an external process.

Coming to terms with polarities is a part of the psychological journey that accompanies maturing as human beings and as artists. In the Classical Ballet technique, opposition is the actual source of our ability to remain on balance in a static pose or to prepare for multiple turns. We reach out in one direction in order to move in the other. Part of the technique is making use of a counter-balance of force, or energy, in order to produce the classical line or movements. This creates the language we use for instruction. Opposition is explicit in the technical training of Ballet dancers. By becoming dancers we process the image of an Ideal archetype. We enter into a sacred tradition if we name God's immanence in creation, God's Becoming. Here is the ancient dialogue of Being versus Becoming, centered in the artistic realm of a highly developed contemporary art form. In Bonaventure's model of synthesis, the question of Being and Becoming (Transcendence and Immanence) is addressed within the theological doctrine of exemplarism. Envisioning the Classical Ballet system as an archetypal Ideal incorporates it into the larger framework of this medieval spiritual tradition. The process of Becoming a dancer is one example of God's immanence in creation which simultaneously points to God's transcendence in the Being of the Classical Ballet Ideal. It seems we have inherited a way of thinking about the Classical Ballet, and experiencing it, that indeed reflects the sacred; or at least the coincidence of mutually affirming complementarity. Either way we are experiencing Transcendence and Immanence, both Being and Becoming.

The earliest primitive ritualistic dances were symbolic language that civilization transformed into a symbolic word system, or religious language. We are exploring the language system of dance in relation to many different symbol systems. Although each symbol system appears to be a separate language in itself, in reality we can apply the diverse languages of many forms of communication to our way of expressing and experiencing traditional art forms. The Classical Ballet has its own symbolic word system in the spoken French language. It identifies the individual steps and series of movements. It also has a whole vocabulary for describing the tension between polarities that creates energy in the technique. These languages merge in the instruction of the Classical Ballet system. The symbol systems of many other disciplines can be another way of exploring dance and placing it in settings that give it broader conceptuality. However, the essence of dance remains in the experience itself. Because the human body is our expressive instrument, the real language is expressed in bodily movements. Symbol systems of words and language are ultimately insufficient means of expressing the experience of dancing, either vicariously, or personally. It is a lived experience, like creativity itself, that eludes our understanding but is recognized in its process.

Our inner journey in life recognizes polarities that appear to need reconciliation. The awakening to awareness of psychic tensions finds artistic expression in the dance. According to Jung, the artistic creative process only appears to be a process of reconciliation. Conscious expression of unconscious archetypal imagery is actually brought about by the unconscious breaking-in to consciousness. Then it is expressed through an artistic medium. The internal and external life journeys are more clearly seen as simultaneous processes in human development. The emphasis is on one or the other at different stages of life. Both modes of consciousness, although specific to one or the other side of the brain, are examples of our coincidence of mutually affirming complementarity. They contain the fullness of potential for growth and development in each of us.

Our circular study places the Classical Ballet system of dance within the framework of sacred tradition and a specific spirituality. Thus we return to the very root of dance; human spiritual experience and religious ritual. At the heart of our philosophy, religion, and art, and at the deepest level of all human experience, a silent pulse of rhythm reverberates like an echo in the universe. That rhythmic pulse is rooted in the heart of the Classical Ballet archetype. Personified in myth through our Psyche, it is theologically grounded in the coincidence of mutually affirming complementarity.

22

The Image of Wholeness

The remainder of this work explores dance in terms of creative unitive experience and transcendence. The three central themes in Bonaventure's system of thought are the Trinity, Christ, and the reflection of God in the universe. Bonaventure was a pioneer of synthesis in his time. His Trinitarian theology gave shape to his system of thought in the same way that the archetypal Ideal of the Classical Ballet system gives shape to the tradition of the Classical Ballet. These three intertwining themes propel us into the centrality of Bonaventure's Christocentric vision. Bonaventure

> sees Christ as the dynamic center of the soul's journey into God, the center of the universe, and the center of history . . . In this dimension, Christ operates as a dynamic center . . . drawing into an integrated whole all the elements of the individual soul, of the physical universe, and of history . . . We can call this a cosmic Christocentricity since Christ is the center of the three major dimensions of the created cosmos: the soul, the physical universe, and history. All lines of the cosmos converge in Christ the center and through him are transformed

and return to the Father. . . . it is precisely the particularity of
the historical Jesus that integrates into an organic and dynamic
energy system the entire cosmos. . . the physical universe,
history, and the spiritual energies of mankind.[1]

The seven chapters of Bonaventure's *Itinerarium mentis in
Deum* (The Soul's Journey into God) is seen as a journey of the
soul toward the ecstasy of mystical union into God. At each of the
seven stages, the reflection of God is seen by Bonaventure in the
symbol of a mirror: ". . . all of creation is a mirror in which God
is reflected."[2] Bonaventure says that he is beginning at the lowest
rung of the ladder of creatures: "Let us place our first step in the
ascent at the bottom, setting the whole visible world before us as
a mirror through which we may pass over to God, the Supreme
Artist."[3]

Bonaventure's stages are drawn from the sixth chapter of St.
Augustine's treatise, *On True Religion*. This describes the beautiful
in direct relation to the laws of numerical proportion, which leads
us to God. Augustine calls these numbers in sounds and voices,
"sounding numbers". Those received by the senses, he calls
"encountered numbers". Those which proceed from the soul into
the body, as seen in gesture and dance, he calls "expressive
numbers". The ascension, step by step, in seven divisions, proceeds
"from the sounding numbers, by means of the encountered, the
sensual, and the remembered numbers".[4]

In the third stage of this inward journey, Cousins continues,

> When we know a first principle, we seem to grasp it in our
> memory since we see it as eternally true, as if we always knew
> it and are now remembering it. When our intellect knows truth,
> it does so in the light of the eternal Truth: and when our will
> desires or judges something as good, it does so in the light
> of the absolute Good. "See, therefore," Bonaventure says, "how
> close the soul is to God, and how, through their activity, the
> memory leads us to Eternity, the intelligence to Truth, and the
> elective faculty to the highest Good."[5]

120

Bonaventure points us in a direction that we experience as artists. It is an inner recognition, or "knowing", a sense of remembering a "truth", or "rightness", in relation to our creative work. Here is an insight into the intuitions, artistic perceptions, and sensitivities in creative activity that we call talent. We describe it as an instinctual knowledge of when we have arrived at just the right movements, or artistic expressions in our interpretations or choreographies. We feel that no other step, movement, or gesture is quite right here. We sense the completeness, or wholeness of our artistic statement. This sense of wholeness, and the symbolism that we associate with it, is the subject of this chapter.

Bonaventure's journey encompasses both the external world of the senses and the internal world of the psyche. Cousins guides us exquisitely into the depth and power of Bonaventure's symbolic imagination. He shows us how Bonaventure's religious symbols serve to enhance his theological and philosophical vision.

> Thus the religious symbol becomes a microcosm for viewing the entire theological-philosophical structure of his thought. It is here that we see the Christological significance of religious symbols. The religious symbol is a microcosm pointing to Christ, the macrocosm...who unites within himself the greatest possible coincidence of opposites."[6]

Cousins reminds us of the importance of Christian symbolism in the history of Western culture, which flowered in the Middle Ages. It was profoundly rooted in a deeply primitive and basic mythological human experience. Bonaventure's principle of exemplarism guides us to his vision of expressionism, which lies at the very core, or center, of the divine life itself. It becomes the ground of all symbolic thinking, reflection, and creativity. For Bonaventure, the expressive core of the divine life is the ground of all human creative experience.

Cousins concentrates on a group of four symbols taken from Bonaventure's system. He explores them from the perspective of the ancient symbol of the mandala. The mandala symbol has surfaced in contemporary Western culture with our increasing interest in meditation and spirituality. I am drawing on my experience of the Mandala principle through years of study, performance, and teaching traditional Classical Ballet.

The four key symbols in Bonaventure are the circle, the center, the cross and the journey. Bonaventure's symbols and system of thought come into a dynamic unity when enlightened by the perspective of the Mandala principle. Mandala, in Sanscrit, means center, or circle. It is an ancient symbol, or design, symbolizing wholeness. Reflected structurally as a cosmic principle of the center, it manifests itself in human consciousness as universal and integrating. It involves polarities, structure, symmetry, all symbolic forms, and the eternal now of time and space. In ancient texts, the center remains as a constant principle. The design, as a circle, symbolizes the cosmos and, as a square, symbolizes the earth, or created world. The Mandala, as a symbol, appears in ritual, art, and religion. It is seen as a basic cosmic structure from the most finite in matter to the infinite in spirit. It symbolizes all levels of awareness, from human beings as individual centers of the universe, to a sacred principle of unity in one eternal center. The design itself is often a circle with a center point, accompanied by a square or cross.[7] As a religious, historical, and ancient symbol, the mandala exemplifies Cousins' understanding of the coincidence of mutually affirming complementarity. Bonaventure's Christocentric view of Christ as the ultimate center exemplifies the mandala in a profoundly revealing way. Likewise, the mandala is the supreme symbol of the Classical Ballet as a technique and an Ideal. First we will describe the symbol, then we will explore its extensive relationship to the Classical Ballet tradition.

Jung researched the mandala as a primitive and natural organizing principle. He discovered it to be the symbol of a universal psychic archetype. The design of circle, or square, symbolizes wholeness. It accentuates the relationship to a central focal point, while inclining towards the pattern, or number, four. Jung identified the number four in his research of dreams and in human cultures as an archetype of total integration. The essence of the mandala is in its healing power. It is a process of harmonizing polarities by centering forces of energy. These forces of energy organize around a center, integrating opposites through the center. They provide a rhythm of passage, away from, and toward, both the source and the goal of created energies. The mandala symbols are representative of the psychic center that Jung identifies with the self in his individuation process. The self encompasses the totality of personality in an integrating, healing process of psychic growth toward wholeness of being. The mandala, for Jung, reflects a basic dynamic structure, or archetype, of the human psyche. In Oriental spiritual traditions, the Mandala principle is both the symbol and the ritual used in contemplation as a dynamic process. It effects the goal for inner transformation by psychic centering as a way of traveling toward spiritual wholeness. Wholeness, in this sense, is related to being able to sustain contact with one's own center. The universality of the mandala symbol in all cultures, from the primitive to the most sophisticated, indicates its life-giving quality. Its presence is a supreme sign of life.

I have been asked, in lecture-discussions, to try to express the inherent "knowing", or intuition of the artist, in creative process. This can never be learned or taught: only nurtured. It must be uniquely experienced by each individual. Our symbolic word systems tend to fumble about in the struggle to find appropriate descriptions of feelings. Enlightened by the Mandala principle, the Classical Ballet system can be described as a formal and structured vocabulary of movement. I have found words that attempt to evoke an inner sense of vision that sees patterns, visualizes movement in space, and captures internally sensed rhythms. Within this self-disciplined training process, a microscopic universe is individually developed. It is experienced as a mini-totality that expands into ever widening circles of increasing inner visual and auditory imagination, enhanced by the sensation of external physical movement. Development of the memory, intellectual capacity, and willpower are mandatory components, but they still cannot command the "talent". We can only nurture the "sensing", "knowing", and the vast potential for "experiencing".

The Classical Ballet system *is* a Mandala principle. The

technical training begins with the centering of the body which we call "placement". It includes training posture which is sustained by strengthening the center of the body in the abdominal muscles and the lower back which support the spine. The alignment of the shoulders with the hips is described as a geometric square at the center of the trunk of the body. This square center supports the movements of the extremities of arms and legs. It initiates and receives the energy of movements which move away, toward, and around the center. The exercises that train the muscles are based on circular patterns of moving the legs and arms. Initially they move around the centered and stationary torso. The body is placed at the center point of a cross from which the legs pass straight through the center first position. Using first the right leg, then the left, the foot points to the front, side, back, and repeat side, making a cross. This pattern is first learned on the floor. The identical patterns are repeated in the air at increasingly higher levels. The arms extend from the center of the cross in similar fashion, held in a specifically oval shape. They circle away and toward the center. When the straight lines passing through the center of the cross are established with the legs and feet, the simultaneous circular patterns of the arms are coordinated. The vocabulary begins to develop the concentric circles that extend in ever larger movements, toward the center and away. Combinations of movements begin to create not only the static postures, but a continuous flow of circular patterns. These become the visual architecture of both the individual's vocabulary and the communal architectural shape of choreographed Ballets.

The entire structure of the Classical Ballet system is based on the circular form with vertical, horizontal, and diagonal lines crossing at the center. We move in eight possible directions. The extremities of the movements of arms and legs always reach to the maximum fullness of the circumference of a circle, touching it at each of its infinitesimal number of points. A photograph of any of the postures, or lines, passed through by the moving dancer, would capture the visual form as a static, sculptured pose. Lines drawn by an artist to fill in and complete the direction toward which the bodily lines or movements point would look like a series of geometrically completed circles in space. Passing through the center, they would circle the sculptured posture, or form, of the dancer's body. Making maximum use of this physically circular, and centered, technique involves the remainder of the Mandala principle.

By establishing a physical center of all potential spatial and visual movement another kind of centering process occurs. It produces a spiritual growing, and psychic integration, that allows the human body to become an instrument of universal and primordial symbolic meaning. The archetype of total integration, that Jung identifies with the number four, is fascinating in the context of the Classical Ballet system. It is not only seen in the structure of the cross at the center of the technique, but also in the musical structure of the training system. The Ballet exercises, corresponding to precise musical rhythm and meter, are based on the number four. The tempos alternate in exercises, from slow to increasingly faster, but the numerical value is evenly structured by counts, and musical phrases, in components of the number four. Dancers begins to feel music and hold or sustain the rhythm. They finally intuit the musical and rhythmical phrasing of movements because of this finely designed structure in the training.

The ritualistic nature and religious self-discipline of the daily training, with the Mandala principle inherent in the Classical Ballet system, meets a very primitive human need to organize our universe around a center. It expresses a fundamental, and dynamic, psychic movement toward wholeness. The Mandala principle stresses remaining in touch with the center, and being consciously present to the now of human experience. I can think of no more concrete, and wholistic, human experience of the eternal now than the experience of the classroom, rehearsal, and performance. In teaching, rehearsing, and performing we must be reminded to remain present. Increasing our awareness of presence and immediacy opens the opportunity for experience. Growth presents itself in the ever-present now in time and space, allowing the Mandala to lead us beyond. I am reminded that I do believe, with Ted Shawn, that "dance has the power to heal, mentally and physically, and that true education in the art of dance is education of the whole person."

125

23

The Lord of the Dance

There are four key symbols which bring a dynamic unity into Bonaventure's system of thought. These are precisely the same symbols that became the root of the Classical Ballet system of vocabulary and technical structure. These symbols are the circle, the center, the cross, and the journey. Reflecting on the history of Western culture reminds us that the Classical Ballet form and technique began to be developed in the courts of Western Europe during the Renaissance period. Therefore, it is not surprising to discover the connection between a system of religious symbols and the construction of a traditional classical art form. The Renaissance period inherited the Christian symbolism of the high Middle Ages. This symbolism is reflected in the various disciplines that were developing in Western Europe at the time. Such symbols are mythologically universal and primordial. According to Jung, they reflect the collective unconscious source of psychic energy that appears in archetypal imagery in every human discipline and dynamic creative process. We have just seen an example of Jung's point in our last chapter. Symbols from the ancient Oriental Mandala

Principle permeate the Classical Ballet system. Cousins envisions the same symbols as a source of dynamic unity in a Medieval Christian spiritual tradition. This parallel establishes a more complete and abundant interpretation for my own experience of the Classical Ballet tradition. The Archetypal Ideal appears to me to have an existential identity and mysterious psychic life of its own.

According to Cousins, Bonaventure's texts explore the theme of Christ as the center. The symbolism is a circle. The center is discovered by intersecting two lines at right angles in the shape of a cross. For Bonaventure, the figure of Christ stands at the center of the circular life of the Trinity. Christ symbolizes a dynamic process of movement in creation. He is both its source and its direction, or goal. Bonaventure experiences Christ as the mathematical center in his own crucifixion, which restores humanity's lost center. Since the cross leads Christ to the resurrection in Christianity, it therefore becomes the supreme symbol of death transformed into life; sin transformed into redemption; and humility transformed into glorification. Christ, at the center of his cross, is the reconciliation of all opposites. He is seen as the center of the self, as well as the center of the cosmos. He is both the goal of the spiritual journey, and the road by which we are to travel. Thus, the circle, the center, the cross and the journey, in juxtaposition with those same symbols in the Classical Ballet system, have a profound connection. Given this specifically Christian interpretation, they come alive with deep spiritual meaning.

We have identified the universality of both the language symbol systems of Bonaventure and the Classical Ballet. However in this specifically Christian context we can clearly point to a spiritual tradition that is likely to have given birth to the Classical Ballet archetype. I identify this archetype with Transcendence, or Being. The archetype, or Ideal, of the Classical Ballet is our means of tapping into a source of creative energy. In Christian terms, we find ourselves at the center of the cross, on the journey toward Self, Christ, and God, in the midst of the circular relationship of the Trinitarian processions. The sacredness at the heart of all traditions is the sacredness in the heart of each unique and creative human life. Christ, at the center, as Self, encompasses the totality of human personality. The center of the cross in the Classical Ballet system becomes the physical center, as well as the spiritual center.

An archetypal image seems to represent both the source of our creative energy, and the goal toward which we strive. In God's Transcendence, personified by the Classical Ballet Ideal, we find the root of God's Immanence in creation, expressed for us through dance. The more we invest ourselves in the process of learning the symbol system of the Classical Ballet tradition, the more deeply we enter into the mysterious life of the dance itself. Dance is one of an infinitesimal number of expressions contained within the eternal reasons by the Word, or Son. Bonaventure sees these expressions of the Son as the ontological ground of every creature. The Classical Ballet becomes an expression of the Eternal Art, or God. Through dance, we find a symbol of wholeness as our center, and the ground of our uniquely individual being, as well. The daily ritual of ballet is our means of physically expressing our psychological and spiritual growing.

The Classical Ballet archetypal image seems to give us life, on the one hand, and entices us to reach beyond that life, on the other. We feel our human limitations because of it, and yet we come deeply into touch with our physical, mental, and spiritual reality within it. The more we enter into the Ideal, the more it enters into us. Because the Classical Ballet system is structurally designed in symbols of wholeness and the integration of polarities, we are physically expressing what we are internally and spiritually experiencing. For me, the Classical Ballet became a means of experiencing the totality of my own personality. Through the archetypal image of the Classical Ballet Ideal, I began my search for Self. Within this system, Jung's individuation process was taking place. All the religious symbols are physically re-created in the daily ritual of centering and placement, and extending circular movements to their maximum fullness. The Ideal was leading me toward a sense of wholeness and of becoming all the components of myself, appropriately. Only here, could I express my inner fragility, and lyrical quality of fluidity in movement. Paradoxically, this happens through a self-disciplined outpouring of energy. The only means to expressing inner sensitivities is through a continuous effort of strenuously building physical strength.

The Lord of the Dance is both Mother and Father, and encompassses both an inner and outward process of giving birth to freedom. By adhering to a strict rule of simplicity and totality, the Ideal is an image of total polar integration. It is as an example of a coincidence of mutually affirming complementarity if it is to truly express the gift of divine life within. In faith, we trust this Mother/Father Lord of the Dance as a means of becoming who we are, and experiencing our relatedness in creation. As our ground of being alive in God, this Mother/Father Lord is a symbol which points us in the direction of where we are to go. In that sense, by falling in love with the Classical Ballet Ideal, we are allowing ourselves to become vulnerable, and therefore open to a call, or vocation. We are becoming enamoured with goodness, truth and beauty. By accepting the invitation to enter into life by means of this synthesis of creative energy we find our artistic self-expression. Dance is our means of communication. We know, deep within, that our love, trust and faith in dance are signs of the gift of life that is an unconditional gift of love. Therefore, the vocation of the artist is parallel to the vocation of the contemplative religious in a very concrete sense. Both are called by Love into loving relationship. They respond to the gift by choosing to surrender to it. By becoming vulnerable, we open ourselves to the meaning of the invitation. It was a humbling experience to choose, and feel chosen to enter into the life of the Classical Ballet. It is the symbolic expression of my own personal life journey. The symbol of that journey, and the experience of the journey, will bring this study to a close. My Contemplative Theory of Dance reaches its fullest expression in the following chapters.

24

The Journey

> The vision and the discipline of the artist is parallel to the contemplation and ministry of the contemplative religious. Revealing a vision to others, the artist is a true contemplative if contemplation is to see what others do not see, and if the artist's ministry is to make visible what he 'sees' and 'knows'. A contemplative is one who sees things for what they really are; who sees the real connections . . . [Contemplation is] a movement from opaqueness to transparency.[1]

Coming to know through experiencing the call of the Classical Ballet Ideal, we enter into a highly developed contemporary dance technique. It is a process that allows us to transcend the vocabulary and be transformed into an instrument of emotional and spiritual artistic expression. Similarly, the spiritual journey of a Christian religious contemplative involves coming to recognize Christ as the center of oneself, others, and the cosmos. This is a process that also allows us to transcend religious vocabulary, and enter into spiritual transformation. All life experience can be described in the light of a journey, or pilgrimage, toward increasingly greater levels of awareness. The journey integrates and processes both our out-ward and inner life experiences. Thus, there is a simultaneous spiritual, psychological, physical and historical life journey that creates our individual stories of human growth and development. These are the components of the journey. Our individual stories reflect a unique and personal response to our own inheritance and life experience. This response gives shape and meaning to our journey.

The purpose of all journeying, according to G.K. Chesterton, is to come home. Each transforming life transition, and every moment of increased awareness, is a part of a continuing conver-sion process. These series of changes are experienced through the dynamics of any of the human disciplines through which we choose to travel. The language symbol systems of our journeys, like all languages, are contained in meaningful symbols, images and myths. From the Christian perspective, we are already alive in God, through Christ. We are called to an awakening and recognition of the divine in all that exists. Our coming to see, as in a mirror, the reflection of God in all of life is the journey described by Bonaventure. We are each invited to embark upon this journey into life. The goal of the journey is transformation.

I feel that I have been invited to travel on many roads at once. I expect that most people exerience life as a journey that leads in many directions and onto many roads. Rarely have I experienced a smooth and freshly paved road, but rather painfully traveled the unpaved, winding, dirt roads of insecurity, uncertainty, and unpredictability. This is often dramatized as the way for all artists. It seems to me, however, to be a very common human experience. Perhaps I am simply reflecting the late twentieth century mind through which my own journey is being lived. According to the latest theory of quantum physics, the natural state of the world, and law of the universe in which we live, is the principle of unpredictability. Just so, a journey into the art and tradition of the Classical Ballet is a choice to make a quantum leap of faith, and begin the pilgrimage home on this particular road. Thus, the beginning of my own journey into the Mystery of creative energy, where art and contemplation meet.

In the Classical Ballet system we travel on a journey from the physical center, through the cross and the circle, in an outward process of learning the technique. The inward process of our journey is a return to the center, in order to express the Ideal. In human psychological growth and development, the initial outward journey can be described as a time of Becoming. The ego develops as our conscious center. We pass through a transitional stage, symbolized by the cross. Entering into the circular dynamics of this integration process, the Self replaces the ego as center of the all encompassing psyche. A dialogue can then be experienced by the conscious ego with its larger and true Self. This is the Jungian individuation process. We are reminded that our mythology symbolically reveals Psyche as a personification of the human soul. Purified by the pain of passion and trial, she is thus prepared for eternal happiness.

In each Christian spiritual tradition, the soul is commonly described as moving through the stages of a journey on its return to God. Bonaventure describes the soul's journey in seven stages. Saint Teresa of Avila also describes the journey through seven mansions in her *Interior Castle*. There is both an outward journey of the senses and an inward journey toward the center, or Christ. In ancient Judeo-Christian Biblical texts, the number seven symbolizes wholeness, infinite number of times, or completeness. The artistic, psychological, and spiritual journeys are simultaneous processes that take a lifetime. By tapping into the Source of creative energy, we discover a life force to endure the journey.

My own journey into the psychic life of the Classical Ballet archetype brings my contemplative theory of dance into life. I am remaining in the spiritual tradition of a journey in seven stages. Utilizing the symbols of the center, the cross, the circle, and the journey itself, I am processing my experience in our twentieth century psychological language system of life transitions. These are the many changes, or conversions, in a lifetime of experience. They indicate the revolving process of growing through becoming into being on many different levels throughout life. Saint Teresa of Avila, a sixteenth century Spanish Saint, and Doctor of the Catholic Church, is my spiritual guide. As founder of the Discalced Carmelite spiritual Tradition, Teresa's *Interior Castle* is an expression of her own spiritual journey. It has become a major contribution to the spirituality of the Carmelite Tradition as it is lived and experienced in religious life today. Entering into the Seven Mansions, or Dwelling Places, of Teresa's *Interior Castle*, the journey of the soul comes alive with imagery and movement.[2]

Teresa uses the image of water symbolically. It expresses the two forms of prayer that she describes in her journey. The first three stages of prayer are active meditation. The fourth stage is transitional. It leads into the infused prayer of the final three stages. In active meditation, we make a conscious effort to pray by using our imagination. We prepare ourselves to recognize God's presence in our lives through the discipline of daily spiritual reading and reflection. In time, we confront our own limitations, distractions, and weaknesses, and enter into a difficult stage of purification. Our moments of peace and inner tranquility begin to lengthen as we enter the experience of infused prayer, or contemplation. We no longer find ourselves working so hard to pump the waters that fill us with life. Instead, the water flows in a continuous stream of life-giving grace.

Teresa's images of water symbolize the interior presence of God. Christians traditionally call upon the living waters of God in prayer and sacraments. The symbols and personifications related to water in primitive mythology strike a familiar chord. Water is a primary life substance that inevitably appears in the legends of our great story ballets. Jung reminds us that water is a symbolic expression, or archetype, of the unconscious movements in the human psyche. Thus, we return to the beginning. The primitive archetypal symbolism and images of ancient tribal rites and ritual reappear in our contemporary artistic expressions. The Classical Ballet Ideal personifies the Mandala Principle. It contains the symbols and images, enclosing them in a free space where we can begin our journey toward wholeness. Teresa's *Interior Castle* also expresses the Mandala Principle, as did the convents she established as symbols of her own inner journey. In the journey into the Classical Ballet Ideal, I began to live the Mandala Principle in the enclosed space of ballet studios. Later, the Mandala lived in the magic synthesis created in the ballets, and performed in the sanctuaries of the theater. The ballet studios, the theaters, and the ballets themselves became expressions of the Mandala Principle. They hold the shape of my story of images, as Teresa's castle contained hers. In both, an inner and outward journey leads to a personal encounter with the divine.

25

The Seven Mansions

THE FIRST MANSION

In the First Mansion, the soul enters into a crystal castle. It is fascinated with the castle, just as I was infatuated with the Classical Ballet when I first began my journey. Something like a warm light attracts the soul. There is a glimmer of recognition. The soul senses a reflection of itself. The Ballets are so beautiful, and it looks so easy. I imagine that I can move like that too. I love the music. It always makes me want to respond by moving and dancing. I am athletic, and take pride in my strong body. I like horses, ice skating and running. The soul is easily distracted by other desires and thoughts of daily activities. But it continues to be drawn to the light. Ballet classes begin to take precedence over other activities. It is hard work, but I am strong and determined. I learn the positions, the shape of the cross, and the circular movements with my arms.

It is the beginning of the journey, and I cannot possibly imagine the whole. Each day, I learn new steps, another part of the daily ritual, and get a little stronger. My body begins to hurt as I force it to make shapes that feel awkward. The music helps. I become more determined and strong willed. Achievement is important. I think that I am learning to control my body, and my life. I think I have found a means to recognition and power. It feels good to work my body so hard. Each day is like a new beginning. I work hard for my teachers, seeking approval for my effort. The soul keeps turning toward the light. It wants to draw near to the source. The ballet studio is spacious, yet crowded with eager, young bodies.

At first, the mirrors at the far end of the studio create an illusion of an even larger space. The images of moving dancers reflected in the mirrors seem to make the room even more crowded. I'm not sure that I recognize my own legs and feet in the mirror. We are divided into three groups. I watch the first group as they seem to confidently dance through combinations of movements. I watch intently, trying to learn the steps and imitate the others, forgetting about the mirror. My body isn't as strong as I thought. I work harder. I imagine how it would feel to turn and jump as easily as the other dancers. Some inner voice insists that I can, and that I will. Listening to the voice, my heart throbs with excitement. I am drawn to that space with the mirrors and barres, like a moth attracted by a light. The light beckons the soul toward the reflection in the mirrors.

THE SECOND MANSION

The soul desires to enter the second mansion. It is drawn toward the room with the light. It hears the call of the inner voice and wants to listen. But the more it hears, the harder it seems to be able to sustain the journey. I listen to the other dancers as they critically observe one another. There is competition in the studio and I am tempted to increase my efforts. I hear the dancers in the Ballet Company talking about musical phrasing, and new ballets to learn. My desire to dance is heightened. I like listening to the dancers. I go to the ballet every night during the season. I watch different dancers perform the same roles, and begin to see the patterns and different interpretations of movements. I am in love with the Ballet.

I return to the studio and look again in the mirror. Is that me? I don't like what I see. The combinations are too hard. I falter and hesitate. I become self-conscious. Maybe I shouldn't dance. I feel the critical eyes of the other dancers watching me stumble. It was easier when I only danced in my imagination. The soul wants to listen to the Word. But it finds itself pulling away from the castle. It is tempted to return to an earlier way of life. It can't go back that easily. My conscience bothers me when I stay away from ballet class. The inner voice calls me back to those awful mirrors. I persevere and resist the temptation to stop. I will try again, today, and tomorrow. The soul keeps turning to the light reflected in the mirror. I want to dance.

THE THIRD MANSION

The soul enters the third mansion. It has learned the daily ritual of prayer and good works. The infatuation is passing. The rewards for living a good life seem small. I go to three ballet classes every day. I continue to struggle with the technique, even when I don't feel any excitement. I'm in the first group now. I know how to see my reflection in the mirror. I criticize my own work, and see when I don't look right. Other dancers watch me now. I work very hard, but I didn't pass the audition today. I think I am as good a dancer as some of those who were accepted. I work even harder than a lot of other dancers. I twist my ankle and have to stop dancing for a while. I feel the insecurity of this life in dance. I was too confident in my own ability. I thought I deserved a reward for my diligence. Others seem to admire my work. The soul learns humility. It knows the light is a reflection of God in the mirror. Only God can say the Word that heals. My effort and achievement are not worthy of praise. No matter how hard I work, I am not yet ready.

THE FOURTH MANSION

I return to the studio to resume my classes. I find I am working my body more gently now. The soul is touched by God. It expands in love. Something new is happening in my work. It flows more easily. I have found my center, and it carries me through the movements. I begin to feel that I am floating along, on top of my work. My legs and feet are strong. My knees cushion the rise and fall of my jumps. I land softly, and jump higher than ever. But the effort is less. My body moves in and out of positions easily. All the movements feel natural. They have become a part of me. I have been touched, and changed, by this training. My body speaks a new language. My images of the patterns and the flow of movements are filled with a new life of their own. I love to dance. My soul moves gently into my dancing. It is the source of my love for dance. It fills my body with energy to express itself through my movements. I sense the internal rhythms, and envision the shapes of whole ballets. I know the music as if I had written it. Every instrument in the orchestra sounds its part in my mind. My soul has been touched by Dance.

THE FIFTH MANSION

I am chosen to dance in the Ballet Company. I surrender to the rhythm of daily class, rehearsals and performances. I am swept along into this new life. Performing is exciting. I feel the energy and sense of community as we join together to make the ballets work. I lose myself in the tremendous exhilaration and intensity of performing. I forget the competition and the criticisms of others. The goal is to achieve a good performance. We work in unison to arouse the applause of the audience. I know when I am "on", and feel when we are pulling together to create a powerful impact. I help another to learn a part. I feel my soul catch fire under the brilliant glow of the stage lighting. Others are touched by my presence on stage. Something more powerful, yet gentle and soft, passes through me to touch others; I know it is there, and that it doesn't belong to me. It is more that I belong to it. In performance, this new life comes alive.

The experience of this new life helps me to want to perform for others. It is no longer my talent. It is a gift that belongs to the community. One of the dancers leaves the Company, and stops dancing. I am shocked. I feel a betrayal. We all feel the loss of one member. After coming so far, I will continue to grow. The effort is all for the sake of the Dance, the whole Company, and the performances. I still feel the awesomeness of the stage. I am privileged to perform on it. Yet, it drains my energy. I lose some of the brightness, and newness. Others catch the fire from my still burning heart. It doesn't matter what I feel. It is what my soul knows, in these encounters. Something dies that is a part of me. And it must die, so that the new can be born. There is no room for complacency here. I must stay awake, if I am to receive the secrets revealed by the Dance. Each encounter with God makes my soul reflect more beauty in every performance. The stage encloses beauty in its free space. Here, energy flows through our bodies and releases in great bursts, reflecting Beauty, itself.

THE SIXTH MANSION

My soul sees clearly that, if it has goodness, it comes from God. It takes great courage to go through the ritual of classes, rehearsals, and performances, day after day. The work is automatic now. I am used to my own reflection in the mirror. Still, I am often surprised that it maintains such majesty, and calm, when I feel such agony. Nothing looks good enough to me. Everything could be better. My love for dance has reached a painful place. I must have patience with myself. I sacrifice everything else for this pain. My soul has felt great joy. It knows the Mother/Father Lord of the Dance. It knows the pain, and the joy. No one's praise or criticism has much effect on me anymore. I have this great desire. I get a physical and painful illness. It seems that God has abandoned me. I can do nothing alone. I wonder if I can love God anymore. Did I truly love Dance? Or was it all in my imagination? Still, I have this overwhelming desire. I don't understand. I'm afraid of myself. I know my limitations and weaknesses well, by now.

My soul takes courage in the knowledge of God's mercy. Who else can give this kind of courage? My body can no longer dance. I know that, through dance, God's Glory is seen in the world. I have great fear and suffer through storms of confusion and unknowing. I live with insecurity. I have mental suffering and physical pain. Only God can calm the storm. I imagine I need the other dancers, the audience, the creative energy of the theater, and the community to praise this Mother/Father Lord of the Dance. My soul hears, "patience". I wait, to enter still another room in this crystal castle.

THE SEVENTH MANSION

Now, I recognize the Source of the warm light that so attracted me when I first entered the ballet studio, long ago. My soul is no longer separated from this warmth. It has drawn me deep into my own humanity. The studio mirror reflects my awakened self. Through this participation and union with Dance I have not lost my identity. Instead, I have become a person, uniquely myself. My soul is more differentiated through this union of opposites. I am united, through the center of Dance, with my own center. I placed my body at the center of the cross in the daily rite and ritual of Dance. But the mirror reflected the other self, where human and divine, art and contemplation, meet. I see that by my limitations and weaknesses, I have received the enabling power and strength of God. How merciful, this Mother/Father Lord who invests so much in me. I have endured the intensity of my own desire, only to find my passion itself is God's own. It is not I who touch other lives, but Dance itself, as it points the way to eternal truth. Grace empowers me to teach, not what I have learned of dance, but rather, what Dance has taught to me. Deep in my heart the rhythms, sounds and movements dance a fountain of living waters. This Source of creative energy, placed in the temple, is waiting to be confronted by the community. "The Lord doesn't look so much at the greatness of our works," says Saint Teresa, "as at the love with which they are done."[1]

In this spirit, I offer the Seven Mansions to all who share this Dance of love, and Life, with me.

Afterword

A REFLECTION ON COMPLETION OF
THE DANCE OF LIFE

I originally conceived *The Dance of Life* to introduce the uninitiated person to dance and the art of the Classical Ballet. In the unfolding process of writing, I discovered that this book is a gift that I wish to offer. It is an experience of dance, grounded in the historical development of human communication, religious expression, and ritual. I am writing out of my own experience of living and dancing in the late twentieth century. *The Dance of Life* is a spiritual, psychological, and philosophical journey. It is an integration of physical and spiritual growing. In my heart, I offer this gift to dancers, aspiring dancers, and all who love the dance. I am privileged to present this book to the global community of all persons. My hope is that *The Dance of Life* reveals the mystery of creative energy. It is this mysterious force of energy that always empowers the next great moment to emerge in the eternal movement of life, and dance.

NOTES

CHAPTER ONE

1. Agnes de Mille, *The Book of the Dance* (Golden Press, 1963), p. 7.

2. Joost Meerloo, *Creativity and Eternization* (Humanities Press, 1968), p. 63.

3. George Leonard, *The Silent Pulse* (New York: Bantam Books, 1981), p. 8.

4. Ibid., pp. 8-9.

5. Meerloo, p. 62.

6. Ibid., p. 69.

7. Ibid. p. 86.

CHAPTER TWO

1. Carl Jung, *Modern Man in Search of a Soul* (New York: Harvest Book, 1983), p. 180.

2. Ibid., p. 181.

3. Marilyn Ferguson, *Aquarian Conspiracy* (Los Angeles: J.P. Tarcher Inc., 1980), p. 108.

4. Ibid., p. 109.

5. Henri Nouwen, *Clowning in Rome* (New York: Image Books, 1979), p. 88.

6. Ferguson, p. 117.

CHAPTER THREE

1. Walter Sorell, *Dance Through the Ages* (Grosset and Dunlap Inc., 1967), p. 17.

CHAPTER FOUR

1. John Martin, *John Martin's Book of the Dance* (New York: Tudor Publishing Co., 1963), p. 18.

CHAPTER FIVE

1. George Leonard, op. cit., p. 13.

2. Ibid., p.17.

3. Marilyn Ferguson, op. cit., p. 109.

CHAPTER SIX

1. Agnes de Mille, op. cit., p. 36.

2. John Martin, op. cit., p. 21.

3. Seyyed Hussein Nasr, *Knowledge and the Sacred* (New York: Crossroad Publishing, 1981), p. 254.

4. Ibid., p. 255.

5. George Balanchine, late founding director and choreographer for our present day New York City Ballet, describes the historical events and personages in chronological order in, *Complete Stories of the Great Ballets,* (New York: Doubleday, 1954). Agnes De Mille (in *The Book of the Dance*) relates the development of Ballet in Europe to the climate of the times. She includes an extensive list of influential personalities.

6. George Balanchine, op. cit., p. 444.

7. Ibid., p. 447.

8. Ibid., p. 544.

9. Ibid., p. 553.

CHAPTER SEVEN

1. Hugo Leichtentritt, *Musical Form* (Cambridge: Harvard University Press, 1951), p. 453.

2. Ibid., p. 454.

3. Walter Sorell, op. cit., p. 118.

4. Silvano Arieti, *Creativity: The Magic Synthesis* (New York: Harper Colophon Books, 1976), p. 237.

5. Ibid., p. 238.

6. Walter Sorell, op. cit., p. 165.

CHAPTER EIGHT

1. Seyyed Hussein Nasr, op. cit., p. 24.
2. Walter Sorell, p. 158.
3. Seyyed Hussein Nasr, p. 148.
4. Ibid., p. 68.
5. Ibid., p. 72.
6. Ibid., p. 75.
7. Ibid., p. 76.

CHAPTER NINE

1. Walter Sorell, op. cit., p. 146.
2. Ibid., p. 179.
3. The growth and development of modern dance is well documented. See Walter Sorell's *Dance Through the Ages*, Agnes de Mille's *The Book of the Dance*, and Walter Terry, *Dance in America*.

CHAPTER TEN

1. George Balanchine, op. cit., pp. 376-377.
2. Walter Sorell, op. cit., pp. 219-220.
3. Balanchine, op. cit., pp. 91-92.
4. Sorell, op. cit., p. 167.
5. *Dance Magazine* (July 1983): 75.

CHAPTER ELEVEN

1. Marilyn Ferguson, op. cit., p. 396.
2. Walter Sorell, op. cit., p. 179.
3. Ibid., pp. 179-180.
4. Walter Terry, op. cit., p. 68.
5. Sorell, op. cit., p. 220.
6. Susanne K. Langer, *Feeling and Form: A Theory of Art* (New York: Charles Scribner's Sons, 1953), p. 173.

CHAPTER TWELVE

1. Marilyn Ferguson, op. cit., pp. 343-344.

2. Carl Gustav Jung, op. cit., p. 152.

3. Ibid., pp. 169-170.

4. Karen Horney, *Neurosis in Human Growth* (New York: W.W. Norton & Company, 1950), p. 332.

5. Ibid., p. 328.

6. Ibid., p. 330.

7. Joseph Campbell, ed., *The Portable Jung* (New York: The Viking Press, Inc., 1971), p. 310.

8. Jung, op. cit., p. 168.

9. Silvano Arieti, op. cit., p. 412.

10. Ibid., p. 414.

CHAPTER THIRTEEN

1. See Agnes de Mille's, *The Book of the Dance*. She describes the work methods of many well-known choreographers.

2. George Balanchine, op. cit., p. 530.

CHAPTER FOURTEEN

1. Joseph Campbell, ed., *The Portable Jung* (New York: The Viking Press, Inc., 1971), pp. 318-319.

2. Huston Smith, *The Forgotten Truth: The Primordial Tradition* (New York: Harper Colophon Books, 1976), p. 40.

3. Campbell, op. cit., pp. 319-320.

4. Silvano Arieti, op. cit., p. 37.

5. Ibid., p. 38.

6. Ibid., p. 27.

7. Smith, op. cit., p. 41.

8. Walter Terry, op. cit., p. 90.

9. Ibid., p. 92.

CHAPTER FIFTEEN

1.   Joseph Campbell, *Creative Mythology: The Masks of God* (Penguin Books, 1968), p. 6.

2.   Ibid., pp. 4, 36, 40.

3.   Joseph Campbell, *Primitive Mythology: The Masks of God* (Penguin Books, 1959, 1969), pp. 70-71.

4.   Ibid., pp. 139-140.

5.   Ibid., p. 55.

CHAPTER SIXTEEN

1.   Joost Meerloo.

2.   Jung, op. cit., p. 172.

3.   Joseph Campbell, ed., *The Portable Jung*, p. 321.

CHAPTER SEVENTEEN

1.   Agnes de Mille, op. cit., p. 40.

2.   Joseph Campbell, ed., *The Portable Jung*, p. 171.

3.   Jung, op. cit., p. 171.

CHAPTER NINETEEN

1.   Henry Paolucci, trans., *Hegel: On the Arts* (New York: Fredrich Ungar Publishing Co., 1979), p.24.

2.   Ibid., p. 37.

CHAPTER TWENTY ONE

1.   See Ewert H. Cousins, *Bonaventure and the Coincidence of Opposites* (Chicago: Franciscan Herald Press, 1978).

2.   Ibid., p. 55.

3.   Ibid., pp. 248-250, 253-254.

4.   Robley Whitson, *The Coming Convergence of World Religions* (New York: Newman Press, 1971).

CHAPTER TWENTY TWO

1. Ewert H. Cousins, op. cit., p. 60.

2. Ibid., p. 79.

3. Ibid., p. 81.

4. Ewert H. Cousins, trans., *Bonaventure* (New York: Paulist Press, 1978), pp. 74-75.

5. Cousins, *Bonaventure and the Coincidence of Opposites*, pp. 82-83.

6. Ibid., p. 162.

7. Jose and Miriam Arguelles, *Mandala* (Shambhala Publications, Inc., 1972).

CHAPTER TWENTY FOUR

1. Henri Nouwen, op. cit., p. 88.

2. Kieran Kavanaugh, O.C.D. and Otilio Rodriguez, O.C.D., trans., *Teresa of Avila: The Interior Castle* (New York: Paulist Press, 1979).

CHAPTER TWENTY FIVE

1. Kavanaugh, op. cit., p. 194.